WOMEN

in the

CBC

Report of the

CBC Task Force

on the

Status of Women

Canadian Broadcasting Corporation

TABLE OF CONTENTS

FOREWORD

At the conclusion of its study, the Task Force on the Status of Women in the CBC made a 2-day visual presentation of its findings, conclusions, and recommendations to the President, Laurent Picard, and senior management. The chapters that follow are a written version of that presentation, and include much of the visual material. We have also attempted to retain the informal tone that prevailed throughout our discussions. While we have had to summarize our conclusions and recommendations, and the discussion that accompanied them, we believe this book is an accurate reflection of the original oral report. The management responses to each of our recommendations are also summarized at the end of the chapters concerned.

At the very beginning of our study, we asked for and received the President's permission to make our findings and recommendations available to all staff. We were grateful for this decision, both because in itself it was evidence of management's support and because we felt that publication was extremely important. Quite simply, we believe that the staff has a right to know how we dealt with the enormous amount of information that many of them helped us to gather, and we are also convinced that a plain lack of awareness of the true situation causes many of the inequities we discovered. As the Task Force found, just being exposed to the facts does make a difference to people's attitudes. So it is our hope that the publication of this report will in itself help the CBC to make some real progress toward ensuring equal opportunity for its female employees.

Acknowledgements

Acknowledgements are due to many individuals and organizations. First and foremost, we should like to express our appreciation to senior management, who took the initiative in setting up the Task Force, gave it a strong mandate, and set aside sufficient funds to enable it to operate efficiently. This is certainly a "first" for the CBC. Aside from the federal Public Service*, we know of no other organization on this continent that has sponsored a study of its treatment of women on the scale of this undertaking.

We owe a special word of thanks to Guy Coderre, Vice-President, Administration, for his support and forebearance throughout. We further recognize and appreciate the very positive response of all senior management to the report itself. The interest and attention with which our presentations were received makes us most optimistic that our efforts will bear fruit.

The six members of the Task Force also wish to acknowledge our debt to our two outside consultants, Florence Bird and Jim Bennett. As Chairman of the Royal Commission on the Status of Women, Florence Bird obviously had a great deal to contribute, both in her knowledge of the Canadian context, and in her experience in leading a team investigating the same

---

*Sex and the Public Service, Kathleen Archibald, 1973.

subject - though on a vastly broader scale. Her expertise as an interviewer (many are familiar with her as "Anne Francis", broadcaster and writer) was also invaluable. She was able to conduct lengthy and probing discussions with senior management while the full-time members of the team planned their tight schedule for the summer months. Throughout, her advice as a knowledgeable and committed "outsider" was much appreciated.

Jim Bennett, a management consultant who had been project leader for the CBC/McKinsey study on human resources management, brought both professional skills and another outside view to bear on the work of the team. He also brought his phenomenal energy and stamina, and encouraged us to set a pace for ourselves that provided a daily challenge. In addition, his presence provided continuity with the human resources management study, and made it possible for us to recommend mechanisms that would fit into future personnel structures.

We are most grateful for the important contributions of both consultants.

The McKinsey organization also provided us with the excellent assistance of one of its editors, Jackie Last, and Sharon Auer, a visual aids specialist, who assisted both in the preparation of the slide presentation and of this report.

We were fortunate to have the part-time services of Elizabeth Gervais, of the CBC's legal department, as our secretary. As well as doing much of our typing and correspondence, she provided an efficient "message centre" during our months of travel. At Head Office, Sheila Jordan also provided many important services.

Arranging for our activities in the cities we visited was a task requiring time, tact, and patience. We are therefore more than grateful to the women who acted as coordinators. They, with the help of senior managers and personnel officers, and often of their Women's Associations, undertook this difficult task, and carried it through with impressive efficiency and remarkably little fuss.

The coordinator role, which proved to be so valuable to the success of our work, had not been included in the original plans. It suggested itself as a partial solution to a problem that arose when women's associations in the West expressed strong objections to the Toronto-Ottawa-Montreal makeup of the Task Force. However, the Task Force members had already been freed from their regular duties, and a larger group seemed likely to be unwieldy. We were anxious to get the fullest possible participation in all parts of the country, and saw the appointment of women coordinators as the solution to obtaining the kind of cross-section of interviewees that we felt was essential. We therefore asked the senior manager at each location we planned to visit to consult with the Women's Association, or with all women employees, and to appoint someone to carry out the coordinator function.

As a result, we had an excellent group of agents in the field. They joined the Task Force in Montreal for a day's briefing at the end of our first week of meetings, and had an opportunity to express the concerns that were uppermost in the minds of the women in their locations. So began a relationship that became invaluable in the course of the summer. Frequent consultations by phone and telex helped to ensure that we would meet with a true cross-section of staff, male and female, management and non-management. We met the coordinators again as our report neared completion, when they served as a test audience for one of the more controversial sections of our presentation. Finally, they came together during the chaos of Montreal's first snowstorm on a cold November weekend, and witnessed the presentation of the complete report.

We should also mention the work of the personnel managers, and many individuals in their departments, who assisted with the gathering of data not available centrally - staff lists, records of absences, training figures. And a special word of thanks to Pierre Racicot, Personnel Officer for Ottawa Area, who had completed arrangements for our meetings there before the coordinators were appointed.

Much of the data we required was, of course, available from Head Office. Our constant demands were met with great patience by Garnett Smith, Don Devlin, John Burns, Dan Danagher, and others.

We received very valuable assistance, as well, from individuals in many outside organizations - Bell Canada, several large banks, the Columbia Broadcasting System, and several Crown Corporations. The Women's Bureau of the Department of Labour, the Office of Equal Opportunities for Women (federal Public Service), the Canadian Labour Congress, and several departments of the Federal Public Service also responded to numerous requests for advice and information. We greatly appreciate their help and interest.

It is never possible to list all the groups and individuals whose efforts have been an essential ingredient in the success of an undertaking such as this. We should like, however, to acknowledge the groundwork laid by the women's associations, and to thank them both for that and for their assistance during the study. And finally - a very sincere vote of thanks to the many hundreds who took time to be interviewed, to join small discussion groups, and to attend our open hearings, and to the senior managers in the locations we visited, who made it possible for many of them to do so.

Discrepancies

The data used in our study were gathered between May and September 1974. Since then, changes may have caused some figures to become out-of-date. For example, in dealing with maternity leave, we used the figure then in effect ($170) as the maximum salary on which unemployment insurance benefits were based, but since January 1975, this maximum has been increased to $185. In addition, because the many computer runs we used for internal data ranged over the whole study period, staff changes reflected in some sets of statistics may not be included in others. Such anomalies are minor, however, and in no way affect the overall picture, or the validity of the conclusions and recommendations of the Task Force.

MESSAGE FROM THE PRESIDENT

The people working for any enterprise are among its most valuable assets, and this is particularly true of a Corporation such as the CBC, whose product is the direct result of the skill, imagination, and motivation of its employees. It is for this reason that we in senior management have been spending a great deal of time and effort in the last year and a half in an attempt to improve the management of our human resources in all its aspects. We have undertaken investigative studies of our manpower recruitment and development, as part of a rather long process of fact-finding and consultation in this area. One important outcome of the early stages of this initiative was the appointment of the Task Force on the Status of Women in the CBC, chaired by Catherine MacIver. This group, appointed last May, has carried out its work with complete independence and with the full support of senior management, and I am happy to say that we are very pleased with the results.

We received the Task Force's findings and recommendations with great interest. Their research made it clear that there have been serious problems affecting women in the Corporation, and we believe they have dealt with each aspect of these problems in a realistic, practical, and convincing manner.

Subsequent to the initial presentation of findings, representatives of corporate and divisional management met - sometimes with members of the task force and consultants - to review the whole program in depth, and to reach decisions with respect to each action recommended. The result of this examination was acceptance in full of 43 of the 56 recommendations, acceptance in principle with certain reservations of a further 12, and rejection of only one. You will find these "management responses" at the end of each of the relevant chapters, separated from the main body of the report in order to preserve the integrity of the argument. As well as indicating management's satisfaction with the work of the Task Force, the very high degree of acceptance demonstrates our firm intention to proceed immediately with the implementation of the equal opportunity program.

The Corporation is committed to this undertaking, and the first specific results will be visible this year. I am sure that when you have read the report you will all agree on the fundamental importance of this challenging new venture, which will affect and benefit all staff, male as well as female. I therefore expect that every staff member will do everything in his or her power to contribute to its success.

Laurent Picard

1. INTRODUCTION

On May 23, 1974, Laurent Picard, President of the CBC, announced the formation of a Task Force on the Status of Women in the Corporation. The Task Force met for the first time on June 17, and made its presentation to senior management 4 months later. The aim of the group was to study opportunities for women in the Corporation, to determine whether inequities existed, and if so, to recommend ways to achieve equality.

BACKGROUND

Throughout the CBC's history, some women employees have been convinced that the Corporation - like most other employers - treated men and women differently. However, it was only in recent years, as society became more aware of problems faced by women in the work force, that the Corporation began to examine its own behaviour in this regard. The first major impetus came from the Royal Commission on the Status of Women, which had undertaken the stupendous task of studying all aspects of the role and treatment of females in Canadian society. Much of the Commission's work was carried out in the full glare of publicity, with coast-to-coast open hearings; its findings and recommendations were eagerly awaited by the many groups and individuals who had participated in the study or had followed its progress through the media. The report was also of great interest to certain organizations that had been examined on behalf of the Commission. Among these were the Crown Corporations, including the CBC. When the Commission reported to Parliament in 1970, it made a number of recommendations especially directed towards these public bodies (Figure 1). It asked, for example, that *"Federal Crown Corporations and agencies (a) develop transfer and promotion measures that will encourage women to move out of the traditionally female occupations into other occupations, and (b) emphasize in recruitment programs that all occupations are open equally to men and women".*

It is not surprising that a number of CBC women, alert to the new opportunities that might open up if this and other recommendations were implemented, armed themselves with copies of the report - and waited for something to happen. When there were no signs of immediate action, some of them banded together to study their situation and to put pressure on management. The first of these associations was a dynamic group of women in Montreal's large French Services Division. The late Judith Jasmin, a distinguished and highly respected foreign correspondent, and Lucille Ayotte, a vital and tireless woman who was also active in CUPE*, brought the Montreal group together in February 1971. Inspired by its activity, a similar group in Head Office (Ottawa) set up shop in January 1973, and Toronto organized in October of the same year. Others followed.

* *Canadian Union of Public Employees*

ROYAL COMMISSION REPORT:
RECOMMENDATIONS TO CROWN CORPORATIONS

43. We recommend that federal Crown Corporations and agencies (a) ensure that women scientists and technologists receive equal consideration with men for appointment, and (b) make a special effort to give graduate women employees a chance to take postgraduate degrees.

44. We recommend that federal Crown Corporations and agencies (a) develop transfer and promotion measures that will encourage women to move out of the traditionally female occupations into other occupations, and (b) emphasize in recruitment programs that all occupations are open equally to women and men.

45. We recommend that each federal Crown Corporation and agency devise a long-term plan for the better use of womanpower within its organization.

46. We recommend that, where the size of staff warrants it, federal Crown Corporations and agencies appoint one or more qualified people whose primary duty for the next 5 to 8 years will be to provide for the training and development of women in their organization.

47. We recommend that federal Crown Corporations and agencies with rotational programs between field and head offices ensure that women are considered for rotation on the same basis as men and are not judged in advance on their freedom to rotate.

48. We recommend that federal Crown Corporations and agencies (a) review their selection procedures to ensure that women are used in recruitment and selection programs, and (b) have senior women officers on their personnel administration staffs.

49. We recommend that different provisions on the basis of sex be eliminated from superannuation and insurance plans for federal Crown Corporations and agencies.

50. We recommend that federal Crown Corporations and agencies (a) make clear to educational institutions, and to the public, that career opportunities within their organizations are open to women and that they are encouraging women to prepare themselves for such careers; and (b) require each private organization with which they do business to include in each contract a clause that prohibits discrimination in employment on the basis of sex.

Fig. 1 The Royal Commission of the Status of Women made recommendations to Crown Corporations in 1970

The women's associations urged management to implement the recommendations of the Royal Commission. To make their case, they collected as much data as they could; they sent out questionnaires, held meetings, and made recommendations. The Montreal group succeeded in getting funds from management to issue a magazine, *Positives,* to bring their activities to the attention of staff and of the press. Later, the Head Office group also received approval to send some of its members across the country to visit other CBC locations and encourage local action.

In the course of their research, the women's groups were able to obtain only a limited amount of hard data. As unofficial associations, they had no access to confidential material. What they were able to get, however, further convinced them that their dissatisfaction was justified. They found, for instance, that while 25 percent of all employees in the Corporation were women, they formed just over 7 percent of management. And there were other, only slightly more subtle, indicators of corporate attitudes. Career brochures seemed to be describing "men" rather than "employees"; and recruiting materials, while they had improved somewhat over the years, still referred to secretaries and script assistants as "she", and to producers, TV production assistants, and managers as "he".

But while many women were convinced of inequities in the CBC, most men did not agree with them. Indeed, a sounding of upper management views elicited statements such as:

> *"Women in the CBC are basically satisfied, as far as I can tell . . . "; "This agitation we're seeing is from a few frustrated women's libbers . . . "; "The Corporation is a leader in giving women opportunity . . . "; "Women have a major piece of the action; look at how many female producers there are . . . "; "The improved education women are getting will take care of things in time . . . "; "On a scale of the CBC's problems, I'd give the women's thing a one or a two (i.e., a very low priority) . . . "; "There's no discrimination in the CBC . . . everyone I know is concerned only with qualifications, regardless of sex . . . ".*

It was obvious that a gulf existed between women's perception of their own situation and the way men viewed it. Clearly, the actual extent and nature of the problem could only be determined by a rigorous study of the facts. Until the situation was analyzed, no effective remedies could be prescribed.

The need for a study began to be evident. The deciding factor was the report in March 1974 of a study of the CBC's overall management of its human resources, carried out jointly by the Corporation and McKinsey & Company, a firm of management consultants. This report underlined the urgency of better management of all personnel, largely because the CBC's "product" - its programs - can only be improved either by a great deal more money, which is hard to come by, or by better and more highly motivated production and support staff. Further, the study group reported that there was unrest - probably justified - among many of the women.

3

Thus, a long process, concentrated mainly in the 4 years since the report of the Royal Commission on the Status of Women, led to the conclusion that no more time should be wasted before tackling the question of equality between men and women. The Royal Commission had concluded that women do not have equal opportunities with men in the CBC. A sizeable number of female employees agreed with them. Most men, on the other hand, believed there was no problem. And finally, a team of CBC officers and professional consultants had identified this area as being in need of immediate attention.

FORMATION OF THE TASK FORCE

And so, on May 23, 1974, the President announced the formation of the Task Force. His announcement included these paragraphs:

POLICY

It is the policy of the CBC that women and men have equal opportunity within the Corporation. Thus, the CBC is committed to a single standard of qualification for employment, and thereafter to equal treatment of men and women in the areas of pay, training, advancement, and prerogatives on the job.

MANDATE

1. Compile information on the situation of women
2. Identify problems facing women today
3. Establish priorities for solving the important problems that are identified
4. Develop specific action programs for each priority area and establish any organizational mechanisms required for implementation.

The Task Force was fortunate in several ways. First, the decision of the President to make this announcement himself went a long way towards convincing the skeptical that the CBC took the matter of equal opportunity seriously. Second, the policy was clearly stated; it was not a question of whether equality was desirable, but of seeking out any evidence of unequal treatment and recommending ways to eliminate it. The mandate was also quite specific; it spelled out the main areas of the Task Force's concern. This made it possible for the work to proceed without delay.

The makeup of the Task Force provided a balance between management and nonmanagement, between French-language and English-language backgrounds, and - with a slight list toward the female side - between men and women (Figure 2).

WHAT THE TASK FORCE DID

The Task Force studied a staff of 10,445 (Figure 3), of whom one-quarter are women and three-quarters men. The 2,650 women have an average age of 35; their average seniority is 7 years; their average salary is $10,090.

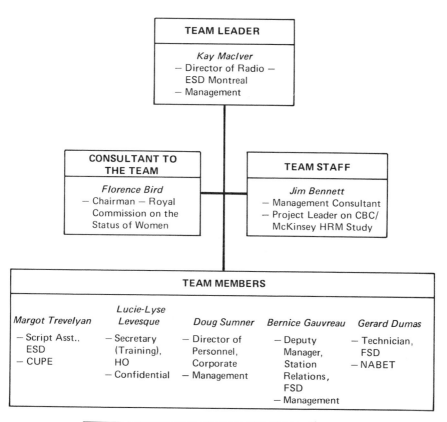

TEAM LEADER

Kay MacIver
— Director of Radio —
ESD Montreal
— Management

CONSULTANT TO THE TEAM

Florence Bird
— Chairman — Royal Commission on the Status of Women

TEAM STAFF

Jim Bennett
— Management Consultant
— Project Leader on CBC/ McKinsey HRM Study

TEAM MEMBERS

Margot Trevelyan	*Lucie-Lyse Levesque*	*Doug Sumner*	*Bernice Gauvreau*	*Gerard Dumas*
— Script Asst., ESD — CUPE	— Secretary (Training), HO — Confidential	— Director of Personnel, Corporate — Management	— Deputy Manager, Station Relations, FSD — Management	— Technician, FSD — NABET

COORDINATORS

Vancouver	Donna Shultz (later replaced by Cathy Little)
Edmonton	Beverly Kelly
Regina	Eileen Hannon
Winnipeg	Eleanor Gajadharsingh
Toronto	Marie Howes
FSD Montreal	Françoise Tremblay
RCI Montreal	Elaine McMaster
EHQ Montreal	Rita Leggio
ESD Montreal	Marièle Choquette
Ottawa Area	Ghislaine Ethier
Head Office, Ottawa	Helen McVey
Quebec City	Hélène Grenier
Moncton	Marie-Reine Martin
Halifax	Barbara McMullin
St. John's	Eileen Dicks

ESD — *English Services Division*
FSD — *French Services Division*
RCI — *Radio Canada International*
EHQ — *Engineering Headquarters*

Fig. 2 The work was carried out by a well balanced team

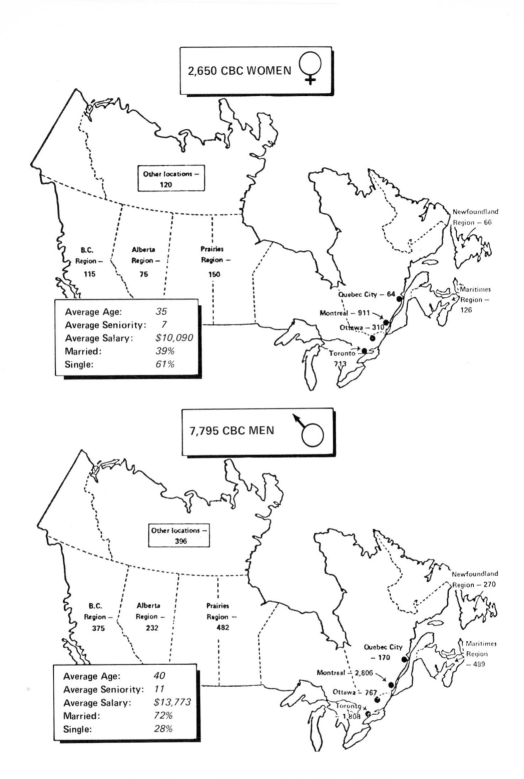

2,650 CBC WOMEN ♀

Other locations — 120

Newfoundland Region — 66

B.C. Region — 115

Alberta Region — 75

Prairies Region — 150

Quebec City — 64

Montreal — 911

Ottawa — 310

Maritimes Region — 126

Toronto 713

Average Age:	35
Average Seniority:	7
Average Salary:	$10,090
Married:	39%
Single:	61%

7,795 CBC MEN ↖⚲

Other locations — 396

Newfoundland Region — 270

B.C. Region — 375

Alberta Region — 232

Prairies Region — 482

Quebec City — 170

Montreal — 2,806

Ottawa — 767

Maritimes Region — 489

Toronto 1,808

Average Age:	40
Average Seniority:	11
Average Salary:	$13,773
Married:	72%
Single:	28%

Fig. 3   There are 2,650 women in the CBC, and 7,795 men

6

Sixty-one percent are single*, and 39 percent married. The 7,795 men have an average age of 40; their average seniority is 11 years; their average salary is $13,733. Twenty-eight percent are single, and 72 percent are married.

Our mandate, then, was to compare the opportunities of one-quarter of the staff with those of the other three-quarters.

Methods

We divided the overall task into an examination of the seven areas that seemed most likely to help us understand the existing situation. These were:

1. *Occupational representation:* Exactly what jobs do women hold, and in which job categories are they not represented? Which positions are *always* filled by women, which are *never* filled by them, and which are staffed by both sexes?

2. *Advancement:* How good are a woman's chances of promotion, compared with those of a man?

3. *Training:* Does the CBC spend as much money proportionately on training women as it does on training men? If not, what are the reasons?

4. *Compensation:* Does the Corporation provide equal pay for equal or comparable work? Do men and women receive the same fringe benefits?

5. *Employment:* How do current hiring practices affect female candidates? What impressions of the CBC's attitudes are left in the minds of women now on staff as a result of their own experiences when they were hired?

6. *Treatment on the job:* How are women treated on a day-to-day basis?

7. *Responsibilities of parenthood:* Some 40 percent of CBC's female staff are married, many with children; how do these women reconcile the demands of parenthood with the demands of the job?

With these seven areas to study, the Task Force had to collect and analyze hard data - the facts and figures relevant to each line of inquiry - as well as to meet as many of the staff as possible in the short time available. And, since even a large sampling of staff would leave out many individuals with something to contribute, we invited written submissions from any individual or group wishing to be heard. We made it clear that both interviews and briefs would be held in strict confidence, unless we had the respondent's permission to make use of the material publicly.

* *Throughout the report, "single" includes divorced and separated people.*

7

By taking this approach, we hoped that the data would suggest areas needing special attention, and that interviews, briefs, and open hearings would reveal impressions and beliefs that could be checked out factually. We expected that the statistics would dispel some myths, and prove some claims. We are confident that this approach was sound.

Apart from research within the CBC, we naturally tried to find out as much as possible about practices in other large enterprises, both public and private, and to consult as many individuals with special knowledge or experience as we could. We talked with placement officers at vocational and technical schools; visited or corresponded with a number of Crown Corporations and several leading Canadian companies; met with representatives of management and women at the Columbia Broadcasting System in New York; interviewed representatives of the Women's Bureau of the Department of Labour, and the Office of Equal Opportunities for Women in the federal Public Service; met individuals from the Treasury Board, and officers of the Canadian Labour Congress. We also gathered, studied, and digested all the relevant research we could lay our hands on.

With all this activity inside and outside the CBC, we correctly foresaw a busy summer. We tried - not always successfully - to arrange our travel for alternate weeks, coming together during the weeks in between to summarize and collate our findings, and to work on data analysis and interviews with outside organizations and individuals. But our most extensive and rewarding activities were the on-location visits in 11 cities, where our agenda included the following:

1. We held individual interviews, lasting 1 or 2 hours each, with a cross-section of all employees - men and women, management and union, in programming, production, operations, and staff services. Our interviewees included young people hired very recently and people on the verge of retirement; those who loved their jobs, and others whose disappointment with their work varied from discontent to bitterness.

2. To include the views of more employees, and to gauge the atmosphere of departments and occupational groups, we also held discussion sessions with groups of three to twelve people - script assistants, clerks, supervisors, secretaries, technicians, engineers, producers - including all-male, all-female, and mixed gatherings.

3. We met with the executive or core group of women's organizations, and held meetings to which all women were invited.

4. Finally, so that no one should be excluded, we invited all employees to open hearings. And, of course, we repeated our request for written submissions from those who did not wish to air their views in public.

As a result of this activity across the country, we managed to meet almost 2,000 staff members in the 2½ months that followed (Figure 4). Having subtracted a generous figure to avoid counting twice those whom we saw both in interviews and at open hearings, we concluded that a modest estimate of individuals seen was 1,974 - an auspicious figure, perhaps.

Altogether, we met with almost one-fifth of all CBC staff. Of the female employees, we met with one-third. We believe that this number of people, so much larger than any opinion poll sample, justifies our generalizing about "opinion in the Corporation".

So - how were we received? What were the reactions to the idea of the Task Force and its work? And how do we, the Task Force members, feel about equality of opportunity in the CBC as a result of so much listening?

Reactions

Inside the CBC, the reaction to the Task Force has been mixed. Many people voiced distrust or skepticism, and a few were either openly hostile or patronizing. One woman wrote about *"the usual fate of most Task Force reports in the CBC - that is to be politely accepted, neatly shelved, and allowed to gather cobwebs"*. We were asked sometimes if the Task Force was not just a front for management. And we often heard people say: *"What! Another Task Force?"*

On the other hand, both written submissions and comments in interviews often expressed hope and goodwill. On the whole, we felt that much of the skepticism disappeared in the course of our discussions.

Outside the Corporation, there has also been lively and growing interest in the project. Newspapers have referred to the study as a landmark, and several large companies, government departments, and universities have expressed a strong interest in receiving the report.

And our own reactions, now that the Task Force has completed its work? First, we do not believe that equality exists; but we think the problem is a complex one, and that there is no single, or simple, solution. Employees do not all agree, and their feelings often run deep. There are vast differences in the way people see the same situation; differences, for instance, between the view of the supervisor and the supervised; between younger and older employees; between senior management and first- and second-line managers. Even within the same groups and organizational levels, conflicting views emerge. For example, not all senior managers agree on the extent or the seriousness of the problem, and not all younger women agree on the CBC's obligations in child care and maternity leave. These differences of opinion are frequently based on fundamental beliefs about the traditional role of women in society, and concerns about the impact of present-day customs and practices on the family as an institution. There are many male employees who firmly believe that woman's place is in the home - or possibly, for a few years before marriage, at a typewriter. There are female employees who accept the stereotype of woman as a passive and obedient

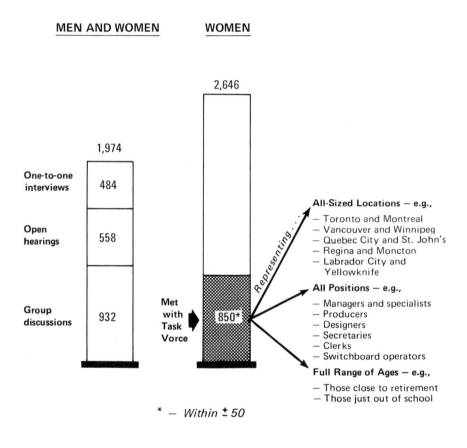

MEN AND WOMEN   WOMEN

2,646

1,974

One-to-one
interviews   484

Open
hearings   558

All-Sized Locations — e.g.,

— Toronto and Montreal
— Vancouver and Winnipeg
— Quebec City and St. John's
— Regina and Moncton
— Labrador City and
  Yellowknife

Representing...

All Positions — e.g.,

Group   Met
discussions with   932   850*
             Task
             Vorce

— Managers and specialists
— Producers
— Designers
— Secretaries
— Clerks
— Switchboard operators

Full Range of Ages — e.g.,

— Those close to retirement
— Those just out of school

* — *Within ± 50*

Fig. 4 On location, the Task Force talked with nearly 2,000 employees, and nearly one-third of the female work force

assistant who should be seen and not heard, and they have little sympathy for the woman who is unwilling to accept that role.

The "women's movement" - within which some include the Task Force - is indeed threatening to many people. There are men who, as one union official put it, have "the depression mentality" and fear loss of their jobs, or of future opportunities for promotion. Others simply fear the unknown, and cannot visualize women as equal colleagues, let alone supervisors. And some women feel their self-image threatened, or fear that association with the cause of equal rights for women will arouse hostility or ridicule on the part of the men in their lives.

To us on the Task Force, these complexities meant that we had to be aware of shadings of meaning, and to guard against the intrusion of our own emotional baggage. We had to try to avoid easy generalizations, and to probe for the facts; to be rigorously objective; and to recognize that it is hard to bring about change.

But we were determined not to take the easy way out. We had to describe the problems as we saw them. We had to insist on the basic principles involved: first, that justice must be done; and second, that our recommendations must contribute to the better functioning of the Corporation, and the welfare of all its employees. Finally, we were convinced of the need to recommend firm but realistic action.

Summary of Conclusions

Our main conclusions, then, were these:

1. Among the majority of CBC women, there is a real and general feeling of discontent about their status in the Corporation.

2. At the root of this discontent are some specific problems, faced primarily by women; the most serious of these is limited access to the majority of jobs.

3. The CBC must take action to solve these problems, both to give its women employees fair treatment and to improve its overall use of human resources.

4. Because such action involves many specific steps and interlocking projects, the CBC should undertake a long-term, comprehensive equal opportunity program, which would do two things:

    a. Demonstrate its commitment by taking *immediate action* in the areas of benefit plans and recruitment, with four specific results to be achieved in a period of 9 months.

b. Thereafter, place top priority on *improving access to all CBC jobs,* through affirmative but noncoercive action.

Leadership in implementing this program should come from an *Office of Equal Opportunity,* to be established immediately. This office would concentrate on programs affecting large segments of staff, rather than following up individual cases of suspected discrimination, and would be headed by a Director answering to the Vice-President, Human Resources*.

5.   The probability that such a program will succeed is, we believe, very high - provided that senior management is committed to it.

In the next chapter of this report, we examine our reasons for concluding that real and general discontent exists, and identify the particular problems that lie at the root of this condition. Subsequent chapters concentrate on each of the main problem areas, and recommend remedial action. We then look at the overall program required to change the situation, and at the procedures and mechanisms that will be necessary to implement it. Finally, we discuss our reason for being optimistic about the success of the actions we have recommended.

These chapters, then, cover our main areas of inquiry. However, two other subjects were also of concern to many of the people we met: the image of women projected in CBC programming, and the status of freelance women. Since neither of these subjects was within our mandate, our observations regarding them are given in an appendix. We also deal briefly in the appendix with three subjects that affect all employees: training, job counselling, and the ombudsman function.

* *We mentioned previously that the personnel and administrative functions in the CBC were the subject of a separate CBC/McKinsey study early in 1974. Certain of the titles that we use in the book - such as Vice-President, Human Resources - anticipate the development of a human resources management structure, as recommended by that study. At the time of writing, this reorganization is in progress at the corporate and divisional levels.*

2. DISCONTENT AND ITS CAUSES

At the outset, the Task Force knew that it would be looking at a wide variety of problems, many of which would be specific to one or other of the seven areas of study. But in addition, there were two broader questions to examine. The first concerns the extent of discontent among women in the CBC. Is it widespread, or is it confined to a vocal minority? The second deals with causes. Apart from specific problems that might be related to advancement or training, for example, are there underlying causes or themes that account for whatever discontent exists?

During our work, the answers to both became clear. To begin with, there is widespread dissatisfaction among women throughout the Corporation. A feeling that women are second-class citizens exists right across the country, though it varies in intensity by location, department, and occupation. While due in part to frustrations common to both sexes, this general discontent is fundamentally caused by their being women in a man's world. For the CBC is a man's world, in that men are in the majority, and hold most of the decision-making power. Men's decisions determine the careers and the working environment of the female minority, and these decisions are based on attitudes that are often quite unlike the attitudes of the women involved. Women's dissatisfaction with this situation is intensified by the fact that they see little prospect of change.

GENERAL DISSATISFACTION

In our field work, we met and talked with almost one-third of all female staff. The 850 women we consulted came from locations of all sizes, as we visited St. John's, Halifax, Moncton, Montreal, Ottawa, Toronto, Winnipeg, Regina, Edmonton, and Vancouver. Women from the smaller centres sent representatives to the nearest cities we visited.

We also met women from all the categories in which the CBC employs them; managers and specialists as well as producers, designers, secretaries, clerks, and switchboard operators. Some of them had been on staff less than a year; others were on the verge of retirement. Among them were a number who were more than happy with their jobs; often they said that the CBC was a much better place to work than other companies with which they were familiar. At the other extreme were a few who seemed to feel that the whole Corporation was in league to make them miserable. In between was the majority, who again and again made comments such as:

> *"All they want to know is if you can type . . ."; "We're watched over like 3-year-olds . . ."; "If they can find space to park our cars, surely they can find a space for our kids . . ."; "There's no place to go if you have a problem . . .";*
> *"There isn't a single female producer here in _____ . . .";*
> *"It's inexcusable that our pension and group life benefits are*

different . . . "; "We're not allowed to think . . . "; "Training? It's non-existent . . . "; "Women are ground down here in ―――― . . . "; "There may be equal pay for equal job descriptions, but not for equal work . . . "; "Supervisors should be given a course to teach them how to treat people; women aren't animals . . . "; and, over and over again, "I was told it was a man's job . . . ".

This feeling of frustration was expressed everywhere, often in almost the same words. However, there were significant variations in the intensity of feeling among locations, departments, and occupations. While we recognize the dangers of generalization, a summary of the variations that we observed is shown in Figure 5. The specific reasons for these differences are many and complex, but they will become clear in later chapters.

UNDERLYING CAUSES

Regardless of the variations in the degree of discontent expressed, the same problems were cited by women across the country: *"little training", "few opportunities for career development", "no job counselling", "poor communications", "bad supervision",* and *"unsatisfying work".* Some of these complaints were certainly heard from men, as well. But in the case of women, the problems assume far greater proportions - partly because women are a minority, and partly because of the very different ways in which women and men in the Corporation view *the role of women at work.*

First, it is important to realize that CBC women are a minority; while there are variations by location, overall they are outnumbered by three to one. There is certainly nothing inherently wrong with a majority/minority situation, but discontent arises when the majority holds a view of the minority opposed to the view the minority has of itself.

Our conversations with employees made it clear that this is indeed the case in the Corporation. To most of the older men, the notion of a woman wanting a career outside the home seemed "unnatural"; in effect, they seem to believe that *"woman's place is in the home".* In contrast, many women hold a quite different view - that *"women should be equal partners in the world of work".*

The wide variation in age and marital status helps to explain why this difference in atittudes exists. Figure 6 shows that whereas almost two-thirds of CBC men are over 35 and married, almost two-thirds of the women are under 35, and single. This means that most CBC men formed their attitudes toward women and their role in society in the rather traditional 1940s and 50s, and sometimes before that. The majority of the women in the Corporation were forming their ideas on the subject in the very different atmosphere of the 60s. The younger men also accepted much more readily the idea of women as equal work partners; many of them assume that their wives will be working for most of their middle years, and contributing to the family income while they do so. Some older men whose wives have reentered the work force told us that they were beginning to see things differently - but we did not meet many whose views were changing in this way.

14

INTENSITY OF DISCONTENT

	By location . . .	. . . by function . . .	. . . and by occupation

Most discontent	EHQ
	FSD Montreal
	Head Office
	Moncton
	RCI
	Regina
		Accounting
		General
		   administration
			Clerks
			MS Is to MS IIIs
			Radio program and
			   production
			   assistants
			Secretaries

	ESD Toronto ESD Montreal Halifax Quebec City Vancouver Winnipeg	Personnel Public relations* Radio programming (French) TV programming	Script assistants TV producers
Least discontent	Edmonton Ottawa Area St. John's	News Radio programming (English)	Radio producers Reporters

* — *Excepting several locations, where discontent is higher*

Fig. 5   *Although discontent exists everywhere, it varies in intensity*

15

CBC men are older . . .   . . . and many more are married

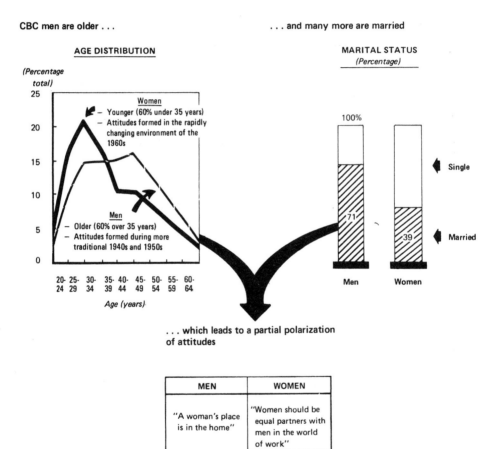

AGE DISTRIBUTION   MARITAL STATUS
                                                            (Percentage)

(Percentage
total)
25

        Women
     — Younger (60% under 35 years)
     — Attitudes formed in the rapidly
       changing environment of the
       1960s

        Men
     — Older (60% over 35 years)
     — Attitudes formed during more
       traditional 1940s and 1950s

20- 25- 30- 35- 40- 45- 50- 55- 60-
24 29 34 39 44 49 54 59 64

Age (years)

100%

71

39

Single

Married

Men   Women

. . . which leads to a partial polarization
of attitudes

MEN	WOMEN
"A woman's place is in the home"	"Women should be equal partners with men in the world of work"

Fig. 6   The male majority seems to hold distinctly different views

16

So women are outnumbered, and their male colleagues generally do not view them as equal working partners; to the Task Force, this partially explained the widespread discontent we had discovered. But we also found that women's frustration was greatly accentuated by the disproportionate power of the male majority over women's careers and working environment. Men in the CBC hold almost all the decision-making power; for example, 93 percent of management personnel are men. Thus, the crucial decisions on employment, advancement, and the assignment of duties for women are made by a majority of men, whose attitudes about women's careers are different from their own.

In a minority-majority situation such as this, it is helpful if one can point to even gradual changes for the better. In the case of the CBC, a comparison of times past and present is not cheering. Whereas until about 1961 the CBC was slightly ahead, both of Canadian enterprise generally and of the (then) Civil Service, in the percentage of women employed (Figure 7), it is now falling farther and farther behind the national average and the federal Public Service. In both of these, women form close to one-third of the work force; in the CBC they constitute only one-quarter of the staff. Further comparisons, to see whether CBC women now hold more positions with decision-making power, provide a picture that is scarcely brighter. There have been slight increases in the percentage of women in producers' jobs and management, but at the present slow rate of change, women would not be proportionately represented in management until the year 2009, (even at the present 25 percent). TV producers would not make it until the late 1990s, and radio producers until the late 80s. In short, things are not "working themselves out", as we were often told. CBC women are well aware that the pace of improvement is slow, and many believe that men are oblivious to their concerns.

In summary, then, the Task Force found that CBC women are discontented, and that there are fundamental reasons for this dissatisfaction. Their "fate" at work is determined by a male majority with very different views from their own, and they see little hope for significant change.

These fundamental causes give rise to a number of specific problems. The first, and most important, is *lack of access to the full range of jobs.* Next is *the situation of secretaries,* who are by far the most dissatisfied group. There are also problems related to *compensation,* including staff benefit plans. Finally, the difficulties women have in reconciling their *responsibilities as parents* with the duties of the job need to be faced and dealt with.

In the following chapters we discuss each of these problem areas, and recommend ways to correct the inequities of the situation in which CBC women find themselves.

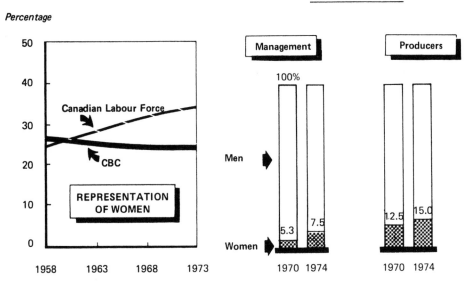

Percentage

Fig. 7 The proportion of women in the CBC has dropped slightly, and their influence is growing slowly

3. JOB ACCESS

Every job should be open to anyone who has the training and ability to do it. As long as positions are closed to any group of people, equal opportunity does not exist.

Even a superficial examination of the CBC would make it plain that many jobs have been wholly or almost completely closed to women, and others have been closed to men. The Task Force set out to measure the extent of "occupational segregation", to study its impact, to look into its causes, and to see what could be done about it.

We began with impressions; from the beginning of our study, we heard from men who thought the CBC was a leader in employing women in interesting and important jobs. *"But look at all the women producers!"* Well - how many are there, in fact? Women, on the other hand, saw themselves as *"mostly secretaries and clerks".* Were they right? How many of the different jobs in the CBC are done by both men and women?

From impressions, we moved to statistics. We studied not only the patterns of segregation, but also their impact on women: what these patterns mean in terms of salary, training, advancement, and decision-making power. These four we will refer to as "corporate wealth". We set out to discover what share women have in this wealth.

In seeking reasons for the patterns that exist, we listened closely to what men had to say about women as a group. It became clear that the majority of them have a set of attitudes that, taken together, forms a stereotyped picture of women, and it was obvious that many of their decisions are based on this stereotype*. That being the case, we tried to test the accuracy of their beliefs. If the picture they have is true for the great majority of women, overall segregation by sex may be justified - and women as a group cannot complain of discrimination, though individual women who do not fit the stereotype may have legitimate grievances. If, on the other hand, the assumptions on which CBC men base their decisions are clearly not true of most women, then women both individually and as a group are the victims of discrimination. We therefore looked very carefully at the various elements of the stereotype and tried to find the evidence that proved or disproved it. This part of our investigation was necessarily less quantitative than many others, but we believe our conclusions are no less valid for that.

As far as job access is concerned, the two most important sets of decisions to be made are those to do with employment, when new staff are being

---

* *Stereotype:*   *"A standardized mental picture held in common by members of a group and representing an oversimplified opinion, affective attitude, or uncritical judgment (as of a person, race, issue or an event)"* - Webster's Third New International Dictionary.

hired from outside; and advancement to more highly paid jobs, from within the Corporation. We therefore needed to examine carefully the ways in which the stereotype influences decisions made by men - who do most of the hiring and promotion - throughout these two processes, before we formed our conclusions and recommendations.

First, the statistics and what they show about occupational segregation.

PATTERNS OF OCCUPATIONAL SEGREGATION

What did the statistics show? We first looked at the positions women now hold in the Corporation. We found that the majority of women - just under two-thirds - are secretaries and clerks in administrative support jobs. Eight hundred and seventy-seven - about one-third - are in jobs related to program production. The remaining 5 percent are in management and specialist positions (Figure 8).

We then looked at the jobs women hold in relationship to the jobs men hold. To determine the degree of job segregation, we defined as *women's* jobs those occupied over 90 percent by women; as *men's*, those occupied over 90 percent by men; and as *integrated*, those in which both sexes are employed, with either men or women holding at least 10 percent of the positions.

We found that most jobs in the CBC are in fact segregated by sex, as is shown in Figure 9, which covers 88 percent of staff, but excludes those positions that employ only a handful of people. Of the 1,425 job titles in the CBC, 1,086, or 76 percent, are "men only" jobs. Some important positions, such as that of producer, film editor, or journalist, appear to be integrated. But women's representation in these jobs is largely confined to central Canada - that is, Toronto, Ottawa, and Montreal (Figure 10). In other words, several of these key positions in other locations are in the "men's jobs" category. Moreover, the number of women in most of these positions is quite small. Had we, for example, used 20 rather than 10 percent as the benchmark for integration, only four occupations would have fallen within the "integrated" category: clerks, computer operators, designers, and radio producers. And had we used 25 percent, only radio producers and clerks would qualify.

THE IMPACT OF SEGREGATION

The Task Force found, then, that the vast majority of CBC jobs are segregated by sex. Our next concern was to determine what impact this pattern has on women's share of the corporate wealth - that is, what they receive from the CBC in the way of salary, training, advancement, and decision-making power.

CURRENT OCCUPATIONS/FUNCTIONS OF CBC WOMEN

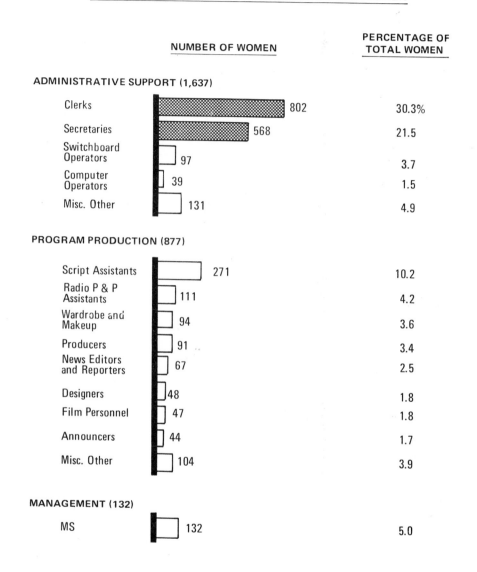

	NUMBER OF WOMEN	PERCENTAGE OF TOTAL WOMEN
ADMINISTRATIVE SUPPORT (1,637)		
Clerks	802	30.3%
Secretaries	568	21.5
Switchboard Operators	97	3.7
Computer Operators	39	1.5
Misc. Other	131	4.9
PROGRAM PRODUCTION (877)		
Script Assistants	271	10.2
Radio P & P Assistants	111	4.2
Wardrobe and Makeup	94	3.6
Producers	91	3.4
News Editors and Reporters	67	2.5
Designers	48	1.8
Film Personnel	47	1.8
Announcers	44	1.7
Misc. Other	104	3.9
MANAGEMENT (132)		
MS	132	5.0

Fig. 8   The majority of women are secretaries and clerks

21

MAJOR CBC POSITIONS*

"MEN'S JOBS" (5,185)

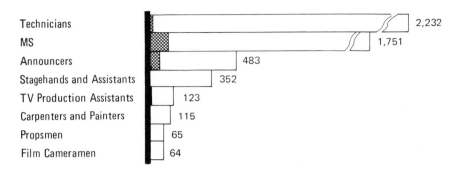

Technicians	2,232
MS	1,751
Announcers	483
Stagehands and Assistants	352
TV Production Assistants	123
Carpenters and Painters	115
Propsmen	65
Film Cameramen	64

"INTEGRATED" ** (2,975)

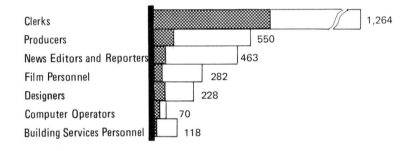

Clerks	1,264
Producers	550
News Editors and Reporters	463
Film Personnel	282
Designers	228
Computer Operators	70
Building Services Personnel	118

"WOMEN'S JOBS" (1,061)

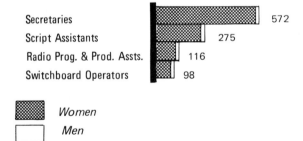

Secretaries	572
Script Assistants	275
Radio Prog. & Prod. Assts.	116
Switchboard Operators	98

Women
Men

* — *Representing 88 percent of all employees*
** — *Women are at least 10 percent of occupants*

Fig. 9   *With the exception of clerks, CBC jobs are largely segregated by sex*

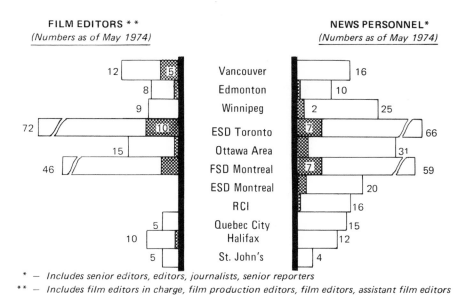

FILM EDITORS * *
(Numbers as of May 1974)

12	5	Vancouver
	8	Edmonton
	9	Winnipeg
72	10	ESD Toronto
	15	Ottawa Area
46		FSD Montreal
		ESD Montreal
		RCI
	5	Quebec City
10		Halifax
	5	St. John's

NEWS PERSONNEL*
(Numbers as of May 1974)

Vancouver	16	
Edmonton	10	
Winnipeg	2	25
ESD Toronto	7	66
Ottawa Area		31
FSD Montreal	7	59
ESD Montreal	20	
RCI	16	
Quebec City	15	
Halifax	12	
St. John's	4	

* — Includes senior editors, editors, journalists, senior reporters
** — Includes film editors in charge, film production editors, film editors, assistant film editors

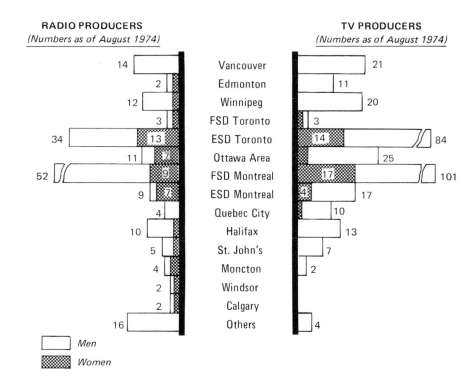

RADIO PRODUCERS
(Numbers as of August 1974)

14		Vancouver
	2	Edmonton
12		Winnipeg
	3	FSD Toronto
34	13	ESD Toronto
	11 / 7	Ottawa Area
52	9	FSD Montreal
	9 / 7	ESD Montreal
	4	Quebec City
10		Halifax
	5	St. John's
	4	Moncton
	2	Windsor
	2	Calgary
16		Others

TV PRODUCERS
(Numbers as of August 1974)

Vancouver	21	
Edmonton	11	
Winnipeg	20	
FSD Toronto	3	
ESD Toronto	14	84
Ottawa Area	25	
FSD Montreal	17	101
ESD Montreal	4	17
Quebec City	10	
Halifax	13	
St. John's	7	
Moncton	2	
Windsor		
Calgary		
Others	4	

☐ Men
▨ Women

Fig. 10 Women's representation in some apparently integrated jobs is largely confined to central Canada

Salaries

In general, "women's jobs" pay less than "men's", as the average salaries for several typical positions show, so it is not surprising that on the average CBC women make over one-fourth less than CBC men (Figure 11)*. Furthermore, this salary difference is significantly greater outside the two network centres and the Ottawa Area (Figure 12).

The fact that some women work for only a short time, and leave the Corporation for marriage or child-raising, might be assumed to account for some of the difference in average salaries. But a closer examination shows that just the opposite is true: at the lowest, or entry levels, women start off at better salaries than men, since "women's" starting jobs usually require a high school education and stenographic skills, while typical "men's" entry level jobs, such as office junior, often require only Grade 10. Thus, men under the age of 20 start off making less than women of the same age, but the crossover starts shortly after this point. Ironically, it is the career woman who sees the gap growing ever wider, until, in the 55 to 59 age bracket, the average woman is making almost one-third less than the average man of the same age (Figure 13).

The effect of this pattern on long-term staff is dramatically shown by a comparison of the work histories and salaries of a group of CBC employees, all of whom have over 29 years' service with the Corporation (Figure 14). Of the 86 in the group, 34 were women, with an average seniority of 32.3 years, and 52 were men, with an average seniority of 33.7 years. Each one entered at the bottom - as clerk 1 or 2, steno, receptionist, switchboard operator, or office boy; we excluded anyone who had entered in a specialist capacity - as announcer, producer, accounting clerk, operator, etc. The women, who had started at an average salary of $893., now make an average salary of $13,476. The men, who started with an average salary of $630, now earn an average of $19,214. And when they retire, the pension of the women in the group will be, on average, 43 percent less than that of the men. In other words, the women have increased their salaries fifteenfold, the men thirtyfold; and the women will have considerably less to live on when they retire.

Training

Sex segregation in jobs has a marked effect on the amount of training an individual can expect to receive, because CBC's training activities are concentrated on positions in which women are not well represented. This is true of internal training activities (Figure 15 gives as an example the French Services Division's 1973 internal training activities) as well as of outside courses of the kind that are fully paid for by CBC. In 1973, for example, Head Office sent 136 men and 2 women on courses (management, planning,

---

* *This refers only to salary, not to overtime; the addition of overtime would increase the difference considerably, since more of the men's jobs involve frequent overtime than do the women's jobs.*

EXAMPLES OF 1974 AVERAGE SALARIES*
(thousands of dollars)

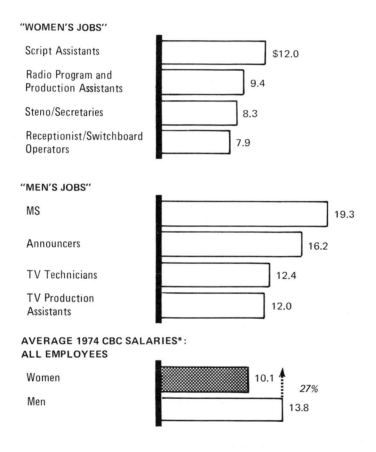

"WOMEN'S JOBS"

Script Assistants — $12.0

Radio Program and Production Assistants — 9.4

Steno/Secretaries — 8.3

Receptionist/Switchboard Operators — 7.9

"MEN'S JOBS"

MS — 19.3

Announcers — 16.2

TV Technicians — 12.4

TV Production Assistants — 12.0

AVERAGE 1974 CBC SALARIES*:
ALL EMPLOYEES

Women — 10.1

Men — 13.8

27%

* — Excluding overtime

Fig. 11   CBC women, on average, make one-fourth less than men

AVERAGE SALARY GAP
(percentage women less than men)

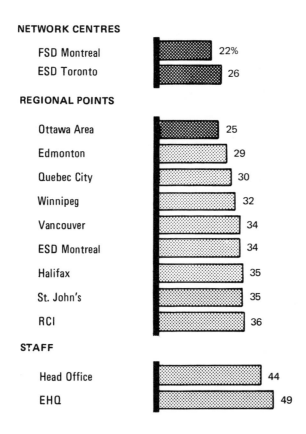

NETWORK CENTRES

    FSD Montreal — 22%

    ESD Toronto — 26

REGIONAL POINTS

    Ottawa Area — 25

    Edmonton — 29

    Quebec City — 30

    Winnipeg — 32

    Vancouver — 34

    ESD Montreal — 34

    Halifax — 35

    St. John's — 35

    RCI — 36

STAFF

    Head Office — 44

    EHQ — 49

Fig. 12   The salary difference is greatest outside the two network centres and the Ottawa Area

AVERAGE CBC SALARIES

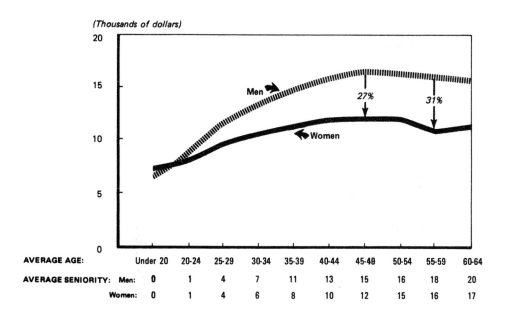

(Thousands of dollars)

AVERAGE AGE:	Under 20	20-24	25-29	30-34	35-39	40-44	45-49	50-54	55-59	60-64
AVERAGE SENIORITY: Men:	0	1	4	7	11	13	15	16	18	20
Women:	0	1	4	6	8	10	12	15	16	17

Fig. 13   The salary gap is worst for women who have made a career in the CBC

SALARIES OF 86 CAREER EMPLOYEES
(over 29 years of service)

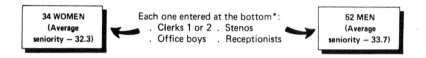

| 34 WOMEN (Average seniority — 32.3) | Each one entered at the bottom*: . Clerks 1 or 2 . Stenos . Office boys . Receptionists | 52 MEN (Average seniority — 33.7) |

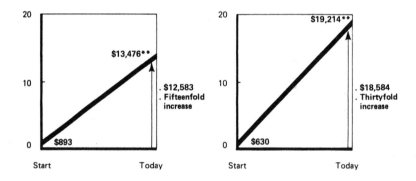

* — *Individuals hired in specialist capacity — e.g., announcers, accounting clerks — were expressly excluded*
** — *At these salary levels, men's pensions will be approximately 43 percent greater*

Fig. 14   A comparison of some long-term employees illustrates the salary gap

FSD IN-HOUSE TRAINING ACTIVITY*
— 1973 —

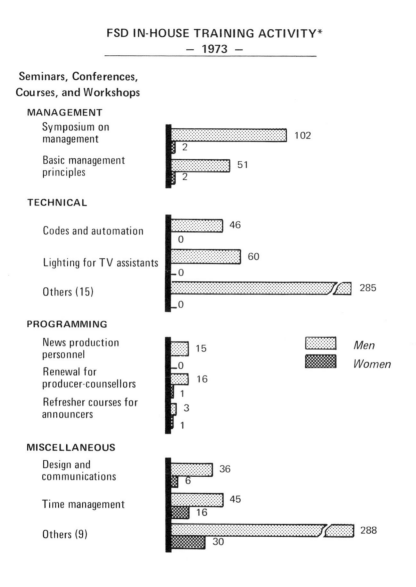

Seminars, Conferences, Courses, and Workshops

MANAGEMENT
Symposium on management — Men 102, Women 2

Basic management principles — Men 51, Women 2

TECHNICAL

Codes and automation — Men 46, Women 0

Lighting for TV assistants — Men 60, Women 0

Others (15) — Men 285, Women 0

PROGRAMMING
News production personnel — Men 15, Women 0

Renewal for producer-counsellors — Men 16, Women 1

Refresher courses for announcers — Men 3, Women 1

Men
Women

MISCELLANEOUS
Design and communications — Men 36, Women 6

Time management — Men 45, Women 16

Others (9) — Men 288, Women 30

* — *Excluding information session on functioning of FSD*

Fig. 15 CBC in-house training activities are concentrated in areas where women are not well represented

computer, duplicating, etc.). Training information from locations covering 73 percent of all staff showed *a woman employee is three times less likely than a man to receive training.* This gap, moreover, varies widely between locations (Figure 16); if you are a woman in Winnipeg or Head Office, you are 30 times less likely to be trained than if you are a man; but if you are a woman in Ottawa Area, English Services Toronto, or St. John's, your chances are closer to being even (though in St. John's in 1973 few courses were available to either men or women).

Advancement

One measure of the way women share in the wealth provided by advancements is quantitative: a comparison of the sheer numbers of transfers and promotions of men and of women. The other and more important measure is the quality of the advancements: into what levels do these promotions bring the employee? Do they really represent steps forward in a career?

Let us deal first with numbers. Statistics concerning the total number of transfers and promotions in the Corporation appear to show that women are doing well. Whereas they make up only 25 percent of staff, they receive over 30 percent of all transfers and promotions (although this varies, and in some locations they receive fewer than 25 percent - Figures 17 and 18).

But when we examine the quality of these promotions, the picture is very different. Looking at Figure 19, we see that men have access to 92 percent of all CBC jobs (the 76 percent classified as "men's" plus the 16 percent "integrated"), while women have access to only 24 percent. So women seeking to advance have only about one-quarter of the alternatives that men have, and certainly the range of options is an important element in the "quality" of advancement.

It comes as no surprise, then, to find that the great majority of the promotions women receive are in the lower paid, traditionally female, occupations - where high turnover creates frequent vacancies. It then becomes clear that their high number of advancements does not mean that women are moving up the ladder into power positions, or even that their range of choices is being significantly increased.

Looking more specifically at promotion at the higher levels, we find that men are three times more likely to advance in "power" positions (Figure 20). This is not surprising, since women hold such a small proportion of these jobs. Again, there are differences between locations, and Figure 21 shows advancements in MS positions in various parts of the country.

Power and Influence

And so women remain a small minority in most positions with influence on policy and programs. Though they form 25 percent of all staff, they hold only about 7.5 percent of MS jobs; 9 percent of announcer positions; and 13 percent of TV producer positions. Only as radio producers are women present in numbers proportional to their total strength in the CBC.

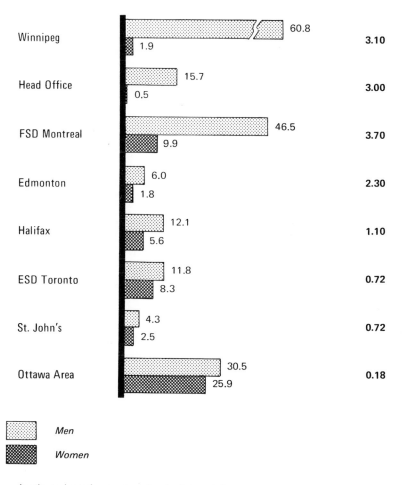

PERCENTAGES OF
MEN AND WOMEN
TRAINED IN 1973*

TRAINING GAP
(Number of times less likely
that women will be trained)

Location	Men	Women	Training Gap
Winnipeg	60.8	1.9	3.10
Head Office	15.7	0.5	3.00
FSD Montreal	46.5	9.9	3.70
Edmonton	6.0	1.8	2.30
Halifax	12.1	5.6	1.10
ESD Toronto	11.8	8.3	0.72
St. John's	4.3	2.5	0.72
Ottawa Area	30.5	25.9	0.18

Men

Women

* — *In those locations returning training data*

Fig. 16   The training gap is overwhelming in a number of locations

31

COMPARISON OF
WOMEN'S REPRESENTATION AND ADVANCEMENTS
(Percentage)

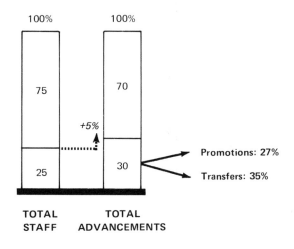

Fig. 17 Women on average get more than their "share" of advancements

32

WOMEN'S ADVANCEMENT OPPORTUNITIES*
(Percentage points between proportion of advancements and proportion of staff)

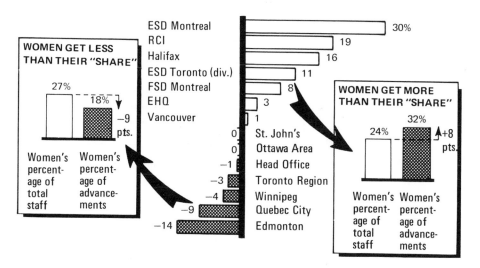

* — Based on 1973 data

Fig. 18 Women's "share" of advancement varies widely by location

1,425 POSITION TITLES

(Percentage occupied by:)

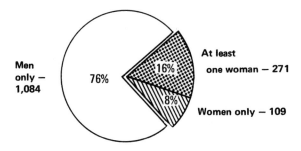

Fig. 19   *Women have fewer advancement alternatives than men*

1973 ADVANCEMENTS
— Producers, Announcers, News Personnel, MS —
(Advancements in these jobs as percentage of total advancements for each sex)

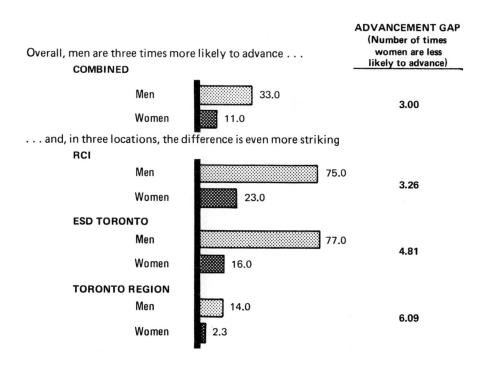

Overall, men are three times more likely to advance . . .

. . . and, in three locations, the difference is even more striking

ADVANCEMENT GAP
(Number of times women are less likely to advance)

COMBINED		
Men	33.0	3.00
Women	11.0	
RCI		
Men	75.0	3.26
Women	23.0	
ESD TORONTO		
Men	77.0	4.81
Women	16.0	
TORONTO REGION		
Men	14.0	6.09
Women	2.3	

Fig. 20   Men are much more likely to advance in "power" positions

35

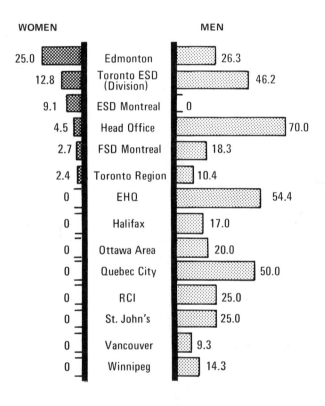

1973 ADVANCEMENTS IN MS

*(MS advancements as percentage of
total advancements for each sex)*

WOMEN		MEN
25.0	Edmonton	26.3
12.8	Toronto ESD (Division)	46.2
9.1	ESD Montreal	0
4.5	Head Office	70.0
2.7	FSD Montreal	18.3
2.4	Toronto Region	10.4
0	EHQ	54.4
0	Halifax	17.0
0	Ottawa Area	20.0
0	Quebec City	50.0
0	RCI	25.0
0	St. John's	25.0
0	Vancouver	9.3
0	Winnipeg	14.3

Fig. 21   Very few women advance in management and specialist positions

These figures do not necessarily represent real "power", as a deeper examination of women in management indicates. For example, 86 percent of MS women are in the bottom three rungs of a 9-rung management ladder that goes up to and includes Director-level jobs. And of all the MS jobs held by women, only 18 percent - 24 out of 132 women - are "bosses" or line supervisors (Figure 22), the rest being in specialist or staff positions. Within the two big network centres, Toronto employs a higher percentage of women in management than Montreal, but both network centres employ a higher percentage of MS women than do any other locations, with the exception of the foreign offices, Northern and Armed Services, and English Services in Montreal, where the numbers are small but proportionately significant (Figure 23).

Taking TV producers as another example, women are often restricted to certain program areas, which may differ by location. In ESD Toronto, for example, very few women produce Entertainment programs. In FSD Montreal, assignments are generally more evenly dispersed, although of the 13 FSD TV specials for 1974/75 that had been assigned at the time of our enquiry, 12 were to be produced by men, and one jointly by a man and a women (final assignment lists for specials within Women's Programs and Music were not available).

In summary, looking at the CBC as a whole we concluded that women do not share equally with men in the "wealth" of the Corporation, because they are restricted to a narrow range of occupations (Figure 24). They are paid one-fourth less money; they are three times less likely to receive training; they have four times fewer advancement options, and are three times less likely to be advanced in power positions. They also hold only a small share of decision-making authority. This is the case throughout the CBC, although the size of the gap between men and women varies considerably from one location to another.

Having established these facts, we turned next to analyzing the causes.

THE SEX STEREOTYPE - TRUE OR FALSE?

Occupational segregation at the CBC developed over a long period of time through a series of hiring and transfer or promotion decisions. Simply put, people get into jobs because they are hired from the outside or are promoted or transferred from within. They do not move into other jobs either because they do not apply, or because they are turned down by the person making the decision. Both hiring and transfer or promotion decisions are heavily influenced by the attitudes of the individual people making the selection, and these same attitudes to some extent shape the processes and practices in use at the present time. Attitudes, in turn, are shaped by beliefs. A fixed set of beliefs about any group is prejudice, from which few, if any, of us are totally free, but application of such a set of beliefs about a group to an individual is discrimination. Most of the decision makers are men. How, then, do the majority of CBC men look upon women as a group?

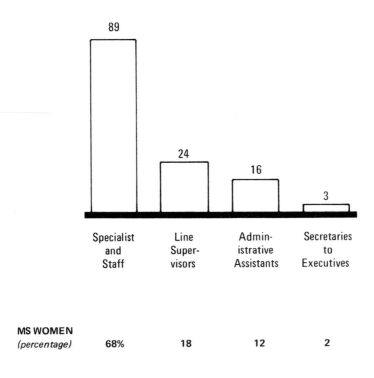

132 MS WOMEN FUNCTIONS OCCUPIED

	Specialist and Staff	Line Supervisors	Administrative Assistants	Secretaries to Executives
	89	24	16	3
MS WOMEN *(percentage)*	68%	18	12	2

Fig. 22   Less than 20 percent of MS women have line supervisory responsibilities

WOMEN'S PARTICIPATION IN MANAGEMENT
(Percentage of MS positions held, as of September 1974)

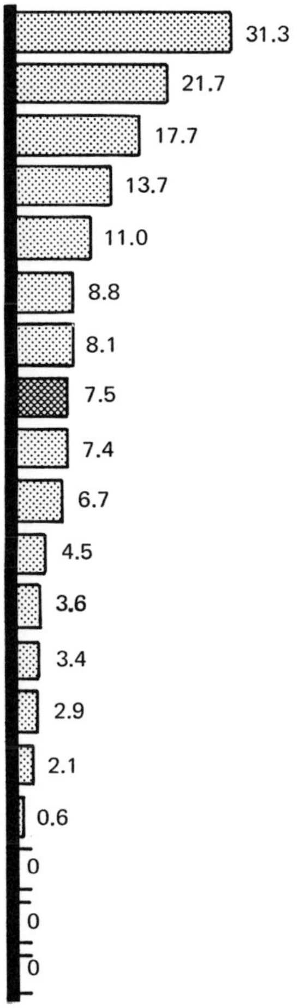

		MS POSITIONS	WOMEN IN MS
Foreign Offices	31.3	16	5
N & AFS	21.7	23	5
ESD Montreal	17.7	17	3
ESD Toronto	13.7	211	29
Toronto Region	11.0	181	20
Head Office	8.8	249	22
FSD Montreal	8.1	418	34
TOTAL CBC	7.5	1,776	132
Quebec City	7.4	27	2
Edmonton	6.7	30	2
ORTO	4.5	44	2
Winnipeg	3.6	56	2
St. John's	3.4	29	1
Ottawa Area	2.9	69	2
Vancouver	2.1	48	1
EHQ	0.6	181	1
Halifax	0	54	0
RCI	0	40	0
Moncton	0	9	0

Fig. 23   Women fare better in management in the network centres than in most regions, EHQ, and RCI

They make one-fourth less money . . .

. . . are three times less likely to receive training . . .

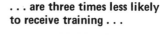

**AVERAGE CBC SALARIES
ALL EMPLOYEES
— 1974 —**

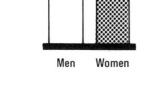

$13,773

$10,090 ⋮ 27%

Men   Women

**PROPORTION OF PEOPLE
TRAINED IN 1973**
(Percentage)

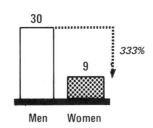

30

333%

9

Men   Women

. . . are three times less likely to be advanced in power positions . . .

**1973 ADVANCEMENTS
— Producers, Announcers,
Journalists, MS —**
(These jobs as percentage of total)

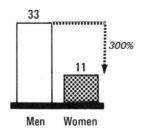

33

11

300%

Men   Women

. . . and hold a small portion of decision-making authority

**REPRESENTATION
OF WOMEN**
(Percentage total in jobs)

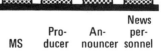

100%

7.5   16.0   8.8   13.0

MS   Pro-
ducer   An-
nouncer   News
per-
sonnel

*Fig. 24   Overall, women do not share equally with men in the wealth of the
Corporation*

40

Our interviews across the country revealed that a good many of the men who do the hiring and promotion at all levels in the Corporation have a very distinctive view of women. While we could cover pages with the observations that were made, in total they added up to a stereotype that is characterized in the four generalizations that we heard most often:

1. *Women are not career-oriented.* They do not expect to get ahead, and would not really want to. They are not willing to move to another city in order to improve their positions. Most of them do not really need the money - or not much.

2. *They are less suited than men for many kinds of jobs.* They do not have the education and experience for specialized or "important" work. They are absent more often. They quit too often. They cannot do strenuous physical work.

3. *They are better suited than men for other kinds of work.* They have greater manual dexterity. They are quick and accurate, and they do not mind repetitive detail as much as men do.

4. *They are overly emotional and generally troublesome.*

If the stereotype painted by these generalizations is true of most women, the job segregation patterns and the resulting gaps in salary, training, advancement, and authority may be justified; and women could complain of discrimination only on an individual basis. If, on the other hand, it applies to only a small number, women are also being treated inequitably as a group, and the CBC is failing to make full use of a quarter of its staff.

We therefore spent considerable time in finding facts to determine whether each element of the stereotype that seemed to be man's view of woman in the CBC is accurate for most women. In some cases, it was possible to find directly relevant data; in others, we had to rely on inferences from other facts; in still others, common sense and observation were the only tools available.

Generalization 1: "Women Are Not Career-Oriented"

1. *"They have no aspirations . . . "; "Women are happy where they are . . . "; "They just want 9:00 to 5:00 jobs so they can get home to their families . . . "; "They're not willing to take the initiative to improve themselves . . . ".*

While the Task Force was unable to find factual evidence to prove directly the extent of women's career aspirations, a number of measures suggest that the majority of women seek careers in the same way that men do. These include the length of time they stay with the CBC; their age; their responses during our interviews; and the results of surveys carried out by women's organizations.

If one assumes that an employee who stays with the Corporation over 5 years is likely to remain with it permanently, it seems that almost as many women as men see themselves as long-term employees, for 80 percent of CBC women and 90 percent of CBC men have over 5 years' service. Length of service does not, of course, necessarily mean that all these employees hope, or wish, to take on ever greater responsibilities, but it does to some extent refute the notion that women are fly-by-night workers, just waiting to get married before leaving their jobs. In fact, 57 percent of CBC women are over 30. One-quarter of these "over 30s" are married, and their average age is 40.6. The average age of the single women in this group is 42.8 (Figure 25).

However, in direct refutation of the statement that women will not work to improve themselves or to advance, data for 1973 showed that, whereas women received little training from the CBC, they were more likely than men to take outside courses* to improve themselves (Figure 26). This was especially the case in St. John's, Halifax, and Toronto, in that order, with Montreal French Services and Ottawa following.

Documentary evidence of women's initiative comes from the returns of two questionnaires sent to all female staff by women's associations in Toronto and English Services and Radio-Canada International in Montreal (Figure 27), in which many women indicated willingness to study to improve qualifications. And evidence from interviews indicated strongly that a large proportion of women do have career aspirations, or at least start out with high hopes. From many secretaries and script assistants we heard statements such as: *"I apply for every production job that comes up"* or, sadly, *"After being turned down four times without ever being given any reason, and seeing the job always going to a young man, I stopped trying".*

2.   *"Women are immobile."*

Although many men spoke of the inability or unwillingness of women to move to another centre, 61 percent of the women working in the CBC are single (Figure 28), and can be assumed to be no less mobile than men. In the surveys quoted above, about 68 percent of the Montreal women expressed willingness to relocate in order to get a better or more interesting job. Some 11 percent were unsure, and only 18 percent would have refused to move. In Toronto, 62 percent of the respondents said yes, 6 percent said maybe, and 32 percent said no. While these surveys do not represent all staff, they contain enough positive replies to rule out immobility as a fact applicable to women as a group. The Task Force also looked at the application forms in the files of 29 TV production assistants (male) and 54 script assistants (female), which show 75 percent of the men and 46 percent of the women to be willing to travel. From this sample, even though more men appear to be mobile, a good proportion of the women are too.

---

* *Courses for which CBC agrees to pay half the costs on successful completion - i.e., all approved as "work-related"*

MARITAL STATUS BY AGE
— 2,646 CBC Women —
(percentage)

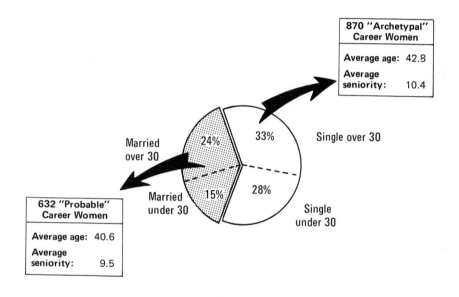

870 "Archetypal"
Career Women

Average age: 42.8

Average
seniority: 10.4

Single over 30

33%

24%

Married
over 30

Married
under 30

15%

28%

Single
under 30

632 "Probable"
Career Women

Average age: 40.6

Average
seniority: 9.5

Fig. 25 The ages and marital status of CBC women argue against the short-term employee stereotype

43

EMPLOYEE'S TAKING "792" OUTSIDE COURSES
(percentage of total employees)

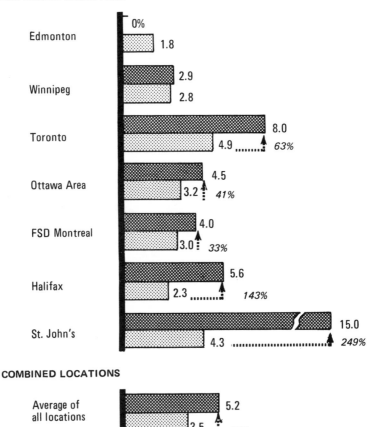

INDIVIDUAL LOCATIONS

Edmonton — 0%, 1.8

Winnipeg — 2.9, 2.8

Toronto — 8.0, 4.9 ... 63%

Ottawa Area — 4.5, 3.2 ... 41%

FSD Montreal — 4.0, 3.0 ... 33%

Halifax — 5.6, 2.3 ... 143%

St. John's — 15.0, 4.3 ... 249%

COMBINED LOCATIONS

Average of all locations — 5.2, 3.5 ... 49%

Women

Men

Fig. 26 Women are more likely than men to take outside courses to improve themselves

44

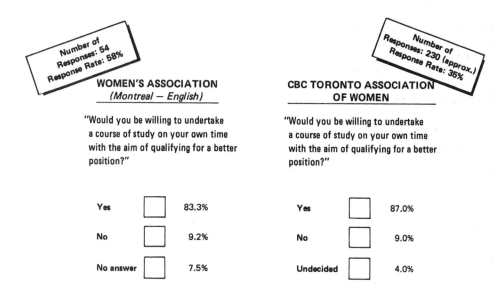

WOMEN'S ASSOCIATION
(Montreal — English)

"Would you be willing to undertake
a course of study on your own time
with the aim of qualifying for a better
position?"

Yes	☐	83.3%
No	☐	9.2%
No answer	☐	7.5%

CBC TORONTO ASSOCIATION
OF WOMEN

"Would you be willing to undertake
a course of study on your own time
with the aim of qualifying for a better
position?"

Yes	☐	87.0%
No	☐	9.0%
Undecided	☐	4.0%

Fig. 27   Women's initiative was documented in returns from two questionnaires

AGE AND MARITAL STATUS
(Percentage employees)

WOMEN

MEN

. Middle-aged: 42.8
. Career woman
. Limited family
  responsibilities
  and ties

Single
over 30

33   24

28   15

Married
over 30

Married
under 30

Single under 30

Married under 30

9   12

63

16

Single over 30

Single under 30

Married over 30

Fig. 28   The large proportion of single women in the CBC can be assumed to be
no less mobile than men

45

3. *"Women don't really work for money."*

Many men think that most women work either to get away from home or to provide a welcome - but unnecessary - second income for the family. This being the case, they conclude that men, who really do need the money, should have preference in hiring and promotions. Some men also assume that the women who work for them are supported by their husbands to the same degree that they support their own non-working wives.

As we have noted before, nearly two-thirds of CBC women are single, and so presumably work to support themselves. Judging from interviews, many of these single people have dependents. Some look after aged parents with small incomes or none at all, while others support children or invalid relatives.

Of the married women (39 percent), roughly half are probably working mothers for whose families the income is a necessity. (Roughly half of all working wives in Canada either have children, or have husbands who make less than $8,000 per year.)

Contrary to the stereotype, then, it seems likely that at least 80 percent of CBC women work out of necessity: 61 percent are single; and probably at least another 20 percent have children to support, or husbands who earn too little to support a household.

Generalization 2: "Women Are Less Suited Than Men For Many Kinds Of Jobs

1. *"They don't have the qualifications."*

Since comprehensive records of individuals' performance and specific work experience have never been kept in the CBC, it is hard to pin down anything other than educational qualifications for most positions. Therefore, in attempting to test the validity of the stereotype, the Task Force looked at educational qualifications and requirements, first in areas from which women seem to be excluded, and then in those where both women and men were represented.

It took little research to find out why there are few female engineers and technicians in the CBC. Engineers need professional qualifications and only a very small number of women graduate in engineering in all of Canada. Although their absolute numbers have increased dramatically since 1969, less than 2 percent of engineering graduates are women, and it is likely that few of these have specialized in broadcast engineering. Technicians must have at least "secondary school graduation, specialized in technically oriented courses or the equivalent", and enrolment figures from technical schools across the country indicate that few women meet the requirements (Figure 29).

Since most other CBC positions do not require specialized training, however, we looked at the general qualifications of men and women in several

ENROLLMENTS IN ELECTRONICS

1970 ENROLLMENTS: COMMUNITY AND TECHNICAL SCHOOLS				
School	Electronics		Radio & TV Arts	
	Men	Women	Men	Women
BCIT	274	2	49	11
N. Alberta Institute of Technology	289	3	39	14
Sask. Technical Institute	147	0	—	—
Geneva CAAT	133	1	48	4
Humber CAAT	41	—	29	22
George Brown	95	—	—	—
Ryerson	611	—	200	105
N.S. Institute	71	—	—	—
College Ahuntsic	223	7	—	—
TOTAL	1,884	13	365	156

1974 ENROLLMENTS: TWO MAJOR MONTREAL TECHNICAL SCHOOLS		
School	ENROLLMENT	
	Men	Women
Techart		
— Day	257	3
— Night	598	2
CEGEP Old Montreal	48	2
TOTAL	903	7

Fig. 29 Up to the present, there have been very few women with suitable qualifications for technical jobs

47

different jobs. In a grouping through which many employees pass at some stage of their careers - CUPE O & Ps*, Group 5 - in Toronto, the women were better educated on average and had a better command of languages (Figure 30). In a sample of script and production assistants, educational levels were roughly equal with more women than men having senior matriculation, but slightly more men having Bachelor of Arts and postgraduate degrees (Figure 31). Both men and women in the sample spoke an average of 1.6 languages; and almost half of the men and the women had production experience outside the CBC. In two other occupations, news reporters and FSD TV producers, a comparison showed little significant difference (Figure 32).

And among people hired in 1974 at the entry level at Head Office, we found that of 13 stenos and secretaries hired, two had degrees (one Bachelor of Arts and one Bachelor of Commerce); two spoke four languages, and one spoke three. Among the six male office juniors hired, none had a degree, and none spoke more than two languages.

Finally, the Montreal English Language Women's Association survey (Figure 33), provides further evidence that CBC women at all levels are well qualified from the point of view of education.

The situation outside the CBC confirms this general pattern. Women now receive nearly half of all university degrees; and the Royal Commission on the Status of Women found that in Crown Corporations female employees were, overall, better educated to high-school level, although men were much more likely to have university degrees than women.

To sum up, the lack of specialized education explains why so few women are represented in several CBC occupations, principally technical jobs and engineering. But for nearly all other occupations, women seem to be at least as well qualified as men from the point of view of education and languages spoken.

2.   "It's a bad investment to promote a woman; she's liable to get married, have a baby, and quit . . . "; "Women are sick and away much more than men . . . I couldn't get the job done . . . ".

As far as "quitting" goes, more women than men do leave the CBC - but usually in the lower paying jobs. The gap narrows in more "interesting" jobs (such as CUPE TV production), and actually reverses in most of the "power" jobs. In MS positions, and among both TV and radio producers, turnover among men is higher than among women (Figure 34). More important than those who leave, however, are the people who stay, and the overall numbers of men and women who stay with the CBC are not very different. Of each 100 men hired, 94 are still there after 1 year; of each 100 women, 87 remain. Seniority figures shown earlier (page 43) further suggest that if women stay for at least 5 years, they probably intend to make their careers at the CBC.

---

* Canadian Union of Public Employees, Office and Professional

EDUCATION OF TORONTO CUPE O & P 5s*
(Percentage having:)

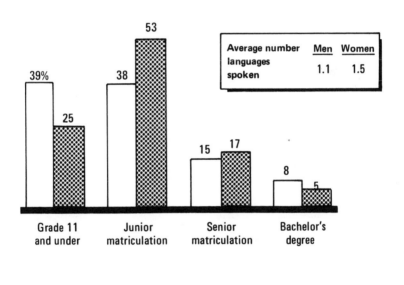

Average number languages spoken	Men	Women
	1.1	1.5

Grade 11 and under — 39% (Men), 25 (Women)
Junior matriculation — 38 (Men), 53 (Women)
Senior matriculation — 15 (Men), 17 (Women)
Bachelor's degree — 8 (Men), 5 (Women)

Men

Women

* — *60 women, 13 men*

Fig. 30 *In a sample of Toronto CUPE O & Ps, women were better educated overall*

49

EDUCATION OF
SCRIPT AND PRODUCTION ASSISTANTS*

(Percentage having:)

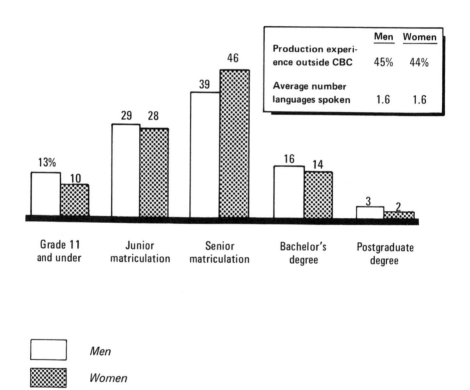

	Men	Women
Production experience outside CBC	45%	44%
Average number languages spoken	1.6	1.6

☐ Men

▦ Women

* — *56 script assistants, 31 production assistants*

Fig. 31 In a sample of script and production assistants, the qualifications of men and women were roughly equal

50

COMPARISONS OF MEN'S AND WOMEN'S QUALIFICATIONS

	NEWS REPORTERS		FSD TV PRODUCERS	
	44 Male	8 Female	65 Male	11 Female
Bachelor's degree	32%	50%	23%	27%
Postgraduate degree	5%	–	12%	–
Diplomas (e.g., teaching)	–	25%	6%	–
Average number languages spoken	1.6	1.8	2.4	3.0
Related outside experience	70%	100%	51%	36%

Fig. 32   *Among news personnel and FSD TV producers, men and women were equally qualified*

RESPONSES TO SURVEY

At what level is your present job?   What is your educational background?

CUPE GROUP	PERCENTAGE OF RESPONDENTS	LEVEL OF EDUCATION	PERCENTAGE OF RESPONDENTS	
1 – 3	11.1%	High school	22.2%	
4 – 5	31.6	College (CEGEP)	11.1	
6	24.1	University	33.3	⎫
7 – 9	14.8	University evenings	18.5	⎬ 61.0%
Producers	14.8	Postgraduate	7.4	⎭
Management		Professional	1.8	
1 – 4	1.8	Business college	5.5	
5 – 9	1.8			
TOTAL	100.0%			

Fig. 33   *The Montreal English Language Women's Association survey suggests that CBC women are a well educated resource at all levels*

CBC TURNOVER IN 1973
(Percentage)

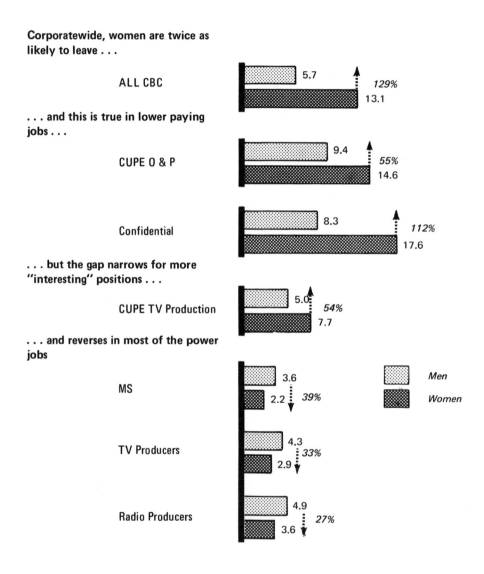

Corporatewide, women are twice as likely to leave . . .

ALL CBC — Men 5.7, Women 13.1, 129%

. . . and this is true in lower paying jobs . . .

CUPE O & P — Men 9.4, Women 14.6, 55%

Confidential — Men 8.3, Women 17.6, 112%

. . . but the gap narrows for more "interesting" positions . . .

CUPE TV Production — Men 5.0, Women 7.7, 54%

. . . and reverses in most of the power jobs

MS — Men 3.6, Women 2.2, 39%

TV Producers — Men 4.3, Women 2.9, 33%

Radio Producers — Men 4.9, Women 3.6, 27%

Men
Women

Fig. 34 Women do leave the CBC more often than men, but not in the more important jobs

52

3. *"They are absent more often."*

True: but the difference is minute. In 1973, for seven major CBC locations, the average number of days worked by men was 216.6 and by women 214.0, out of a year of 225.0 working days. The difference is 1.2 percent.

4. *"Women are unable to do strenuous physical work . . ."; "A woman couldn't climb up a ladder with those lights . . ."; "Women can't stand cold temperatures; can you imagine one at the top of Mount Orford taping a ski race . . .".*

The average man is considerably stronger than the average woman. Studies differ a great deal in their conclusions about just how much stronger; an American research project set the difference at about 30 percent, while a similar British study put it as high as 80 percent. Since physical strength depends not only on heredity, but also to a great degree on regular muscle use, such variances may result from differences in the habits of the men and women in the particular community where the study is done. However, all such studies point out that individuals vary enormously; and at the extremes of the scale, we find very strong women and very weak men. Nor are the numbers of strong women insignificant; physiotherapists, who are mostly women, have to have great strength, as do nurses in old people's homes who must often lift 200-pound men without assistance. Farm women who do outdoor chores also develop strong muscles, and so do women who regularly take part in active sports.

Thus, both outside research and observation indicate that while, on average, men are indeed stronger physically, a sizeable minority of women are quite as strong as the average man, and many women do hold jobs requiring physical strength. Some women, like some men, do not want to do heavy physical labour, and they are unlikely to apply for jobs that require it. To paraphrase John Stuart Mill, if certain jobs are too tough for women, they are hardly so stupid that one needs to make rules preventing them from taking such work.

As for their ability to stand the cold, we first heard this particular comment on the very day that two young women were engaged in swimming some 30 miles in the chilly waters of Lake Ontario.

Generalization 3: "Women Are Better Suited For Some Jobs"

1. *"They are better with their hands . . ."; "Women are much more suited than men for switchboard operators, because of their nimble hands . . ."; 'They have the manual dexterity it takes for typing; men don't . . ."; "I wouldn't mind having a woman in my department (technical), if I could get a position that combined tape editing and typing . . .".*

Outside research suggests that this assumption is wrong. Of eight studies of inherent manual dexterity that we looked at, four found that men and three found that women have greater dexterity; one found no difference between the sexes. Manual dexterity is also, to a considerable extent, acquired through practice; many technicians, for instance, may be more deft than many women clerks.

2. *"Women have more patience with dull jobs . . . "; "They're good as accounting clerks: faster and more patient . . . "; "Women don't mind repetitive jobs . . . "; "She can last better at a job that tends to mono- tony; she's used to thinking about other things while she does the housework . . . "; "Men are born wanting a life of challenge; women are not born with this want, and that's why they are happy to be just secretaries . . . ".*

On the contrary, turnover tells its own story; women quit lower paying jobs at a rate twice that of men. And our interviews uncovered a reservoir of discontent among women in repetitive jobs. The Task Force therefore con- cludes that this belief, widely held and often repeated, is ridiculous.

Generalization 4: "Women Are Overly Emotional And Generally Troublesome"

An extreme expression of this view came from one supervisor of a largely female staff: *"I have a lot of women working for me, and they're quite good. But they cry so much."* (He didn't know why, and felt that to ask would be *"too personal". "Don't they always cry?"*) Women saw things somewhat differently. *"If a woman cries - usually through sheer frustration with the impossibility of getting through to her boss - she's unstable and a nuisance. If a man shouts, he's a gutsy guy."*

Obviously, the Task Force had great difficulty in finding data to prove or disprove the statement that women are overemotional and generally trouble- some. So we had to rely on observation and common sense. It seems to us that both men and women are emotional, but generally show their emotions in different ways. Women do occasionally cry. Men are more likely to shout or be aggressive. What is unfortunate is that men and women frequently have only a limited understanding of the way in which the other sex reacts, and may be embarrassed or frightened by any outburst.

In summary, the Task Force concludes that much of CBC men's stereotype of women either has little relevance to "doing the job" or is simply untrue. Our findings on the truth or untruth of each assumption, and on its relevance to performance on the job, are tabulated in Figure 35.

We have considered the elements composing many men's idea of the "typical woman" at some length, because within the CBC it is the men who do most of the hiring, promoting, and transferring. Their decisions have resulted in the present pattern of occupational segregation, and the consequent unequal distribution of corporate wealth, which we have already described. We will now take a closer look at just how the stereotype influences these decisions, starting first with employment and then moving to advancement.

SUMMARY OF STEREOTYPE

AREA	ELEMENT	Relevance to Job Performance			Degree of Validity About the Majority				COMMENTS
		High	Medium	Low	True	Some Truth	Very Little Truth	False	
Not career-oriented	Limited aspirations			▨				▨	• Large majority of CBC women desire advancement
	Unwilling to relocate			▨			▨		• CBC women are less willing than men, but at least half appear pre-pared to travel or move
	Little need for money			▨				▨	• At least 80 percent of CBC women work out of necessity
Less suited than men for many jobs	Less qualified	▨				▨			• CBC women are less qualified for technical and engineering jobs • Qualifications for others are equal to or greater than men's
	More often absent		▨				▨		• CBC women are present only 1 percent fewer days annually than men
	Quit too frequently		▨			▨			• CBC women's turnover is higher, but not in important jobs
	Unable to do strenuous physical work		▨			▨			• Although men are stronger on average, some women are stronger than some men
Better suited for other positions	Greater manual dexterity		▨					▨	• Outside research says no inherent difference; dexterity is acquired
	More tolerant of detail			▨				▨	• Interviews with CBC women and turnover data suggest the exact opposite
Overly emotional	Too frequently cry			▨			▨		• Both men and women express their emotions, but in different ways

Fig. 35 Much of CBC men's stereotype of women either has little relevance to doing the job or is simply untrue

55

THE STEREOTYPE AND EMPLOYMENT

In considering the influence of the stereotype on employment decisions, it is first important to realize that hirings from outside, because they are so large in number, have a major impact on occupational segregation. For example, in 1973, 850 people, some 8 percent of the total staff, joined the Corporation (Figure 36). Moreover, this annual number is likely to double in the near future, since an estimated 8,000 new employees will be required over the next 5 years to fill a staffing gap caused by growth on the one hand, and turnover and retirements on the other (Figure 37). It is therefore clear that the sex of the new employees will have a tremendous impact on the future pattern of segregation.

The sex distribution of new staff in each occupational group will to a large degree determine the occupational patterns "up the line" as well as at entry levels because of the career paths employees often follow (Figure 38). For example, union agreements require that certain positions be filled from within the bargaining unit, provided there is a candidate with the minimum specified qualifications. To steal a phrase out of context from historian Frank Underhill, we will continue to suffer from "hardening of the categories" unless we change our traditional hiring practices.

For both these reasons, the Task Force felt it important to determine where and how the stereotype affects employment (Figure 39). Unfortunately, we found that it works to the disadvantage of women at each step in the employment process, from finding candidates right through to the final selection.

Finding Candidates

There are many ways of finding candidates. They include newspaper advertising, distribution of recruitment materials to schools and universities, keeping in touch with placement officers at technical and vocational schools, and informal enquiries among friends and colleagues. With the exception of newspaper advertising, which we found to be generally free of references to sex, the stereotype is at work in all these methods of recruitment.

We could scarcely believe some of the pamphlets and films that the CBC, in the year 1974, was still distributing to schools and universities. Many pamphlets carefully describe sex-stereotyped roles, as the excerpt from *Careers in the CBC* shown in Figure 40 indicates. Another version of this brochure is even more explicit. It explains that the job of film librarian *"is better suited to a man because handling of heavy materials is part of it"*. These "heavy materials" are cans of film, which female script assistants carry every day, in considerable quantities and for long distances.

A second example of the stereotype at work comes to light in two films intended to inform students about careers in the Corporation. An English-language film, produced some years ago in Toronto but still in regular use, shows women carrying coffee, "helping" the producer, and typing, typing, typing. Wayne and Shuster, the hosts, are in their usual gleeful form; their

DISTRIBUTION OF 1973 HIRINGS
BY SEX AND LOCATION*

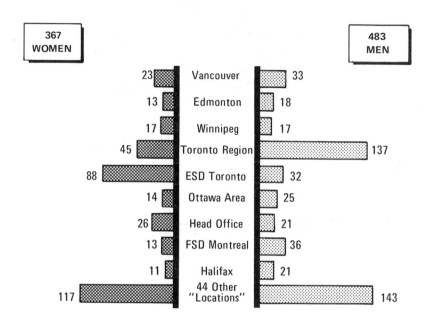

367
WOMEN

483
MEN

	Women		Men	
Vancouver	23		33	
Edmonton	13		18	
Winnipeg	17		17	
Toronto Region	45		137	
ESD Toronto	88		32	
Ottawa Area	14		25	
Head Office	26		21	
FSD Montreal	13		36	
Halifax	11		21	
44 Other "Locations"	117		143	

* — *Excludes 705 temporaries and summer reliefs
(438 men and 267 women)*

Fig. 36   Large numbers of people are hired annually by the CBC

CURRENT AND PROJECTED
CBC STAFFING
(Number of people)

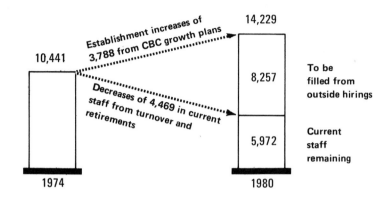

14,229

10,441

Establishment increases of 3,788 from CBC growth plans

Decreases of 4,469 in current staff from turnover and retirements

8,257 — To be filled from outside hirings

5,972 — Current staff remaining

1974   1980

Fig. 37   Over 8,000 people must be hired from the outside from now to 1980

SEVERAL TYPICAL CAREER PATHS
(From samples of CBC work histories)

EXAMPLES

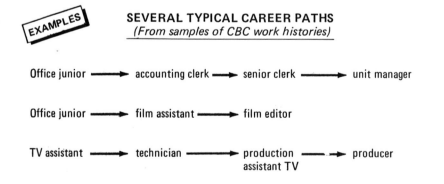

Office junior ⟶ accounting clerk ⟶ senior clerk ⟶ unit manager

Office junior ⟶ film assistant ⟶ film editor

TV assistant ⟶ technician ⟶ production assistant TV ⟶ producer

Fig. 38   Some typical career paths illustrate the importance of entry level jobs

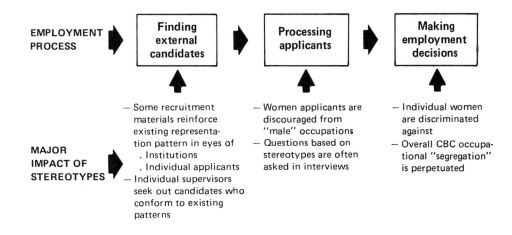

| EMPLOYMENT PROCESS | Finding external candidates | Processing applicants | Making employment decisions |

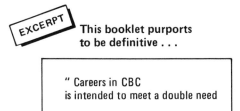

MAJOR IMPACT OF STEREOTYPES

— Some recruitment materials reinforce existing representation pattern in eyes of
 . Institutions
 . Individual applicants
— Individual supervisors seek out candidates who conform to existing patterns

— Women applicants are discouraged from "male" occupations
— Questions based on stereotypes are often asked in interviews

— Individual women are discriminated against
— Overall CBC occupational "segregation" is perpetuated

Fig. 39   The stereotype affects each step of the employment process

EXCERPT

This booklet purports to be definitive . . .

" Careers in CBC is intended to meet a double need

Increasingly, young people about to come on the labour market need exact information about the careers available to them when they complete their studies

Employment counsellors often consult our personnel services to get information on job opportunities in CBC

Thanks to this booklet, both groups now have available a clear and simple description of the different trades and occupations used in broadcasting"

. . . But sex stereotypes most jobs

— 48 jobs for men — e.g., "The producer must have a solid artistic background. He must have an appreciation of all forms of art . . . "

— 6 for women — e.g., "Production Assistant is the title of the aide whom the producer engages as assistant in the preparation and production of radio programs. In the producer's absence, she directs rehearsals . . . "

— 13 that are for either — e.g., "The sales representative is entrusted with . . . The holder of this post . . . "

Fig. 40   Pamphlets currently in use describe sex-stereotyped roles

commentary includes: *"We have GIRLS, too . . . girls to file, girls to type . . . GIRLS . . . just to brighten our day!",* and *"Girls don't* make *records, they* file *them!"* At one point in the movie, the duo peep surreptitiously over a wall divider, leer at the women working below, and exclaim, *"We have to start spending more time at the office!"*

The French-language film, a more recent production and an otherwise excellent one, also reinforces the idea that women are carrying on a fairly exclusive love affair with their typewriters. Neither film carries the message that women do, even now, hold some key production and management positions.

Recruitment materials, then, reflect and reinforce many elements of the stereotype, such as women's inability to do physical work, greater manual dexterity - on the typewriter - and, by implication, lack of aspirations. Small wonder, then, that another source of external candidates - the placement officers at technical schools, community colleges, and CEGEPs* - revealed in interviews that they are by no means aware of the CBC's stated equal opportunity policy. Most officers had seen the CBC recruitment materials, but they usually have only informal and irregular contact with the Corporation. This contact is occasionally with employment personnel, but more frequently with line supervisors. *None of the placement officers with whom we spoke view the Corporation as having full job access for women.* Thus, our recruitment materials clearly discourage female students from applying for any but the traditionally "female" jobs, and discourage guidance counsellors from suggesting that they prepare for other careers in the CBC.

A third, very common method of finding outside candidates is through enquiries among friends and colleagues. A supervisor with a vacancy to fill may spread the word among business, academic, or social acquaintances. Our interviews led us to believe that, consciously or unconsciously, they often search for people who fit the current mold; if a man has held the job, they look for a man, and *vice versa.*

Screening

While it is evident that so far in the recruitment process the stereotype tends to channel women toward traditional occupations, the most serious obstacle to breaking away from those occupations is the screening process. We found evidence that the woman who does apply for a non-traditional job is likely to be in for a painful experience. Active discouragement, impertinent questions, and condescension frequently await her.

A sampling of statements from interviews and briefs illustrates how women are discouraged from aspiring to jobs usually held by men:

* *Collège d'Education Générale et Professionelle*

"I was told it was a man's job . . . " (This we heard again and again, in relation to many occupations); *"When I applied to Radio-Canada the choice was limited . . . secretary or script assistant . . . ";* *"He* (the employment officer) *didn't ask me anything about the kind of work I was interested in, or what my education or experience was. He just wanted to know if I could type . . . ".*

So we see again the "manual dexterity" and "lack of aspirations" stereotype in operation.

In addition, some women reported that they were asked questions, which, at best, can only be described as irrelevant: *"Why would a pretty girl like you want to be a producer?".* And there are comments such as *"Come on, now . . . your boyfriend wouldn't like you going out of town with an all-male crew!",* and *"Built the way you are, you'd distract the guys in the studio".*

Other questions are undoubtedly intended to obtain relevant information, but are put in personal rather than professional terms. Women think it unlikely that male candidates are asked detailed questions about personal circumstances, and few questions about their education and work experience. Questions such as *"Are you married? Have you any children? Do you plan to have a baby? What does your husband (father) do?"* are frequently posed. From the answers to questions about marriage and family, supervisors are likely to make assumptions based on the stereotype; for instance, they may assume that a married woman will not be able to do overtime or shift work, or that she will be unable to take a job in another city. More relevant and specific information can, women believe, be elicited by asking questions directly: *"Are you prepared to work evenings or weekends, should the need arise? Are you free to travel? Would you be willing to move to another city?"*

Condescension, even ridicule, though probably unintended, is another repeated complaint of the woman applicant. *"I felt patronized when I was told that the job wasn't suitable for a woman. I'm capable of deciding for myself whether or not a job is too physically demanding."* Again, an assumption has been made on the basis of a belief about women as a group.

Hiring

When it comes to the actual hiring decision, the Task Force found that CBC policy is clear, but is often honoured in the breach. The statement of policy includes the unequivocal declaration that:

> **"The Corporation, within its means, will seek out and secure the most qualified candidates for openings that occur".**

In its guidelines on application of this policy, we read that:

> **"The officer in charge of personnel is responsible:**
>
> **— For screening applicants to ensure they meet the conditions of employment**

61

— For providing supervisors with assistance and guidance in the selection of candidates.

THE SUPERVISOR SHOULD CONSULT HIS SUPERIOR, OTHER SUPERVISORS CONCERNED, AND THE OFFICER IN CHARGE OF PERSONNEL TO ENSURE THAT THE FINAL DECISION IS ACCEPT-ABLE AND IN LINE WITH ALL REQUIREMENTS FOR EMPLOYMENT" (Capitals ours).

In actual practice, supervisors in some locations have wide latitude to make decisions. Very often, the personnel officer is merely a rubber stamp; and equally often, the supervisor making the decision consults no one. Under these circumstances, his version of the stereotype can and frequently does rule the choice.

Most of the discriminatory decisions - that is, decisions based on a group stereotype, accurate or inaccurate - that we encountered may have been unconscious or unintended. Sad to say, we found a good number of instances where such decisions were conscious and deliberate. Some men as well as women told us of male colleagues who say openly that they would never hire a woman for certain jobs. Some men told us so directly, or said, *"I'd be willing to hire a woman if a really capable one applied. But frankly, I've never met a capable one."* And a few said they would hire a woman only if the position were changed to include typing, so making use of her supposed "manual dexterity". One or two admitted that women can do certain "male" jobs well, but said they would feel uncomfortable if they ever had to discipline them.

The overall consequence of these employment practices - finding outsiders, screening, and making employment decisions - is shown in actual hirings in 1973. Of a total of 850 employees hired, only 86 men and 78 women were hired in positions where the opposite sex was also hired; most of the women in this group were hired as secretaries and clerks (Figure 41). Taking Head Office, Toronto, and Montreal as specific examples, a distinct pattern emerges (Figure 42). The Corporation is still hiring along traditional lines, so that employment decisions today are reinforcing occupational segregation rather than breaking it down.

THE STEREOTYPE AND ADVANCEMENT*

There are even more transfers and promotions than there are hirings from outside the Corporation; 1,593 in 1973, compared with 850 new hirings. So it is clear that advancement decisions have even more impact on the segregation patterns than do employment decisions. As with employment, the number of opportunities will rise with expansion and retirements (Figure 43).

---

* Advancement is used here to mean a promotion to a higher job level or a transfer to a different position in the same job level accompanied by a salary increase.

NUMBER OF HIRINGS IN 1973

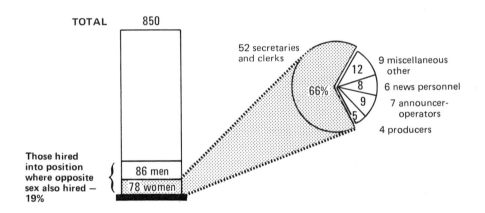

Fig. 41 *Only a few hirings involved both sexes, and most women in these categories were hired as secretaries and clerks*

HIRINGS IN 1973

	TORONTO REGION		ESD TORONTO		HEAD OFFICE		FSD MONTREAL	
	Men	Women	Men	Women	Men	Women	Men	Women
"TRADITIONALLY MEN'S JOBS"								
Management	5	0	9	1	10	0	7	2
Technicians	60	1					11	0
Announcers	1	0						
Film cameramen	1	0						
Building services personnel	8	1					7	0
TV production assistants	3	0						
Stagehands and designers	10	0					1	0
Chauffeurs	3	0						
Total	**91**	**2**	**9**	**1**	**10**	**0**	**26**	**2**
"INTEGRATED"								
Film personnel	8	1	1	1				
News editors and reporters	4	1	10	0			3	0
Clerks	30	17	8	2	0	5	1	2
Makeup and costume personnel	0	3					0	4
Producers	0	0	4	2			1	0
Total	**42**	**22**	**23**	**5**	**0**	**5**	**5**	**6**
"WOMEN'S JOBS"								
Secretaries	1	14	0	61	0	16	0	3
Switchboard operators	0	2						1
Script assistants	0	5						
Radio program and production assistants			0	1				
Total	**1**	**21**	**0**	**62**	**0**	**16**	**0**	**4**

Fig. 42   Hirings in Toronto, Head Office, and Montreal illustrate the corporate pattern

64

PROJECTED VACANCIES TO 1980
IN "IMPORTANT" JOBS TO BE FILLED BY
INTERNAL PROMOTION OR OUTSIDE HIRING

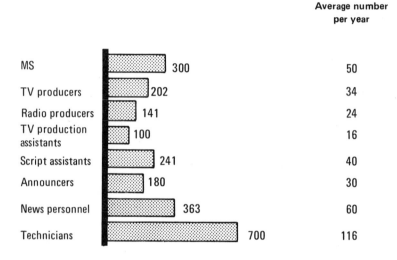

Average number
per year

MS	300	50
TV producers	202	34
Radio producers	141	24
TV production assistants	100	16
Script assistants	241	40
Announcers	180	30
News personnel	363	60
Technicians	700	116

Fig. 43   To 1980, many vacancies will arise in "important jobs"

It is then doubly unfortunate that unfairness in advancements is the single most frequent complaint the Task Force heard, from both men and women. However, we found that, while both sexes suffer, women are relatively much worse off because of the way the sex stereotype affects each step of the process (summarized in Figure 44). Women who had sought promotion were bitter about their experiences:

> *"They always promote someone in from outside the depart-*
> *ment . . . when people internally are clearly qualified . . .";*
> *"The job is always filled before the posting goes up; every-*
> *body know that, so why bother . . ."; "Promises, prom-*
> *ises . . ."; "Why is it so much more glamorous to come from*
> *outside the CBC than within . . ."; "It's who you know that*
> *counts . . ."; "No one even had the decency to tell me why*
> *I was turned down . . .".*

Identifying Candidates

Present methods of finding candidates within the CBC are inclined to be haphazard. There is a certain amount of planning within some departments, but systematic manpower planning across the Corporation is in its infancy. This affects all staff, but women are especially handicapped because they are simply not thought of for "men's jobs".

Jobs at the lower levels* are at least posted and, with all its inadequacies, the posting system is of some help to women. It does give notice that the opening exists, and the recently adopted practice of including the statement that *"This position is open to both men and women"* - though still not consistently used - is a reminder both to the selecting supervisor and to the female employee that her application must at least be acknowledged, and that it cannot be dismissed by the statement, *"This is a man's job".*

Because neither available inventories nor posting procedures have proved dependable, supervisors rely on more informal methods of finding people. They look among those they know personally - inside and outside the Corporation - and resort to the "old boy network" if there is no obvious choice at hand. Being in the right place at the right time takes on a lot of meaning. So when the job is not posted, women are far more likely than men to be completely ignored. If the woman applicant is in a different department or location, her very existence, not to mention qualifications, may be unknown. And the old *boy* network is not likely to draw attention to her as a potential candidate. Judging from our interviews with supervisors, the decision maker frequently assumes that the position will be filled by a man because the former incumbent was a man.

Sometimes, of course, women are considered at the outset, but in the present system they may be eliminated without even being aware that they were on

---

* *All union jobs and those MS I to MS IV that entail supervision*

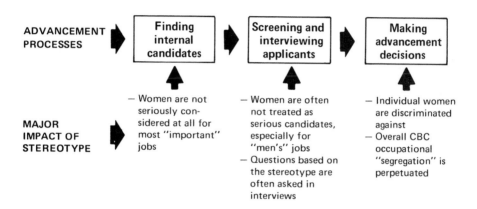

ADVANCEMENT PROCESSES → **Finding internal candidates** → **Screening and interviewing applicants** → **Making advancement decisions**

MAJOR IMPACT OF STEREOTYPE

— Women are not seriously considered at all for most "important" jobs

— Women are often not treated as serious candidates, especially for "men's" jobs
— Questions based on the stereotype are often asked in interviews

— Individual women are discriminated against
— Overall CBC occupational "segregation" is perpetuated

Fig. 44   As with employment, the stereotype affects each step of the advancement process

67

the initial list. The decision maker may make any number of assumptions about their willingness to take the job: that they wouldn't *"want to move . . . be able to travel . . . want the responsibility . . . like to work with all male colleagues . . . be accepted as a boss".*

Screening Candidates

Let us suppose, however, that the female candidate does get on the list of candidates to be interviewed. The Task Force found that this process is often less than effective for both men and women. The requirements may not be precisely defined; the supervisor may not be really sure of what he is looking for. Selection boards may or may not be used; if they are, they may not include the appropriate people, and may operate without proper guidelines. Very often, supervisors conduct the whole process largely on their own, and the questions may reflect their bias, or simply fail to elicit information relevant to the job. This lack of system is more damaging to women than to men, because - as quotations from briefs and interviews illustrate - the candidate's sex seems to assume more importance than her qualifications.

> *"If you want a man's job, you'd better go to Toronto with the rest of the smart-ass broads . . .";* *"Why do you need the money - you make a good salary now . . . "* (echoing again the stereotype); *"That's really a man's job . . . "* (with reference to unit manager, TV production assistant, cameraman); *"When I want a production assistant with big boobs, I'll let you know . . . ".*

Making Decisions

Given the attitudes expressed in these screening interviews, it is not surprising that at the time of making final choices women applicants are often ruled out. Stereotyped ways of thinking largely explain the patterns of occupational segregation above the entry levels, particularly in the power positions. These prejudices frequently result in decisions that discriminate against individual women, and perpetuate the status quo.

Sometimes discrimination is unconscious and unintended; unfortunately, as with employment, we encountered a number of instances in which such decisions were deliberate. Interviews with several men made it clear that they would be willing to promote only a very exceptional woman, though they freely admitted that they believe in taking a chance on a man who appears to have potential. Others simply could not imagine a woman in a supervisory position, though they usually insisted that this was not a result of personal prejudice, but a belief that other employees would not be willing to work for a woman.

The fact that women do get many advancements at the lower levels, but seem to be blocked at the levels that would lead to lower and middle management positions, seems to be both the result of stereotyped thinking and the cause of the lack of qualified female candidates for senior posts. While promising men often get the opportunity to move up the job ladder in a way that prepares them for ever increasing responsibilities, this steady progression is rare among women. Until advancement decisions are based on qualifications, rather than on a set of fixed beliefs, there is little hope that segregation at the upper levels of management will come to an end.

CONCLUSIONS

In summary, our study of the extent to which women have access to jobs in the CBC revealed several things. The majority of jobs are at present closed to women. In the case of some specialized categories, this is because few women have the requisite education, but for the most part, their restriction to a relatively narrow range of functions is a result of employment and advancement decisions made on the basis of a set of assumptions about women that are demonstrably untrue of the majority. And as a result of the narrow range of jobs they hold, women do not share equally with men in the corporate wealth.

The Task Force therefore concludes that *women in the Corporation are treated inequitably as a group.* It follows that *individual women are frequently the victims of discrimination,* since the decision makers often make judgments about the capability of an individual woman on the basis of characteristics they associate with women generally, and act on those assumptions to deny women access to many categories of work.

We also conclude that by denying women access to the full range of jobs, *the Corporation also loses in a number of ways.* The pool of candidates for any job is considerably reduced by excluding one or the other sex, and the best candidate may be in the excluded group. Valuable abilities simply go to waste, and the different perspective that women can bring to many positions, particularly in program production, is frequently lost. Talented women may become frustrated and leave; in the early and mid-60s, for example, several women who had been unable to advance beyond the lower supervisory levels left for managerial positions elsewhere. Some women whose abilities might be valuable to the Corporation may see most of the more challenging jobs occupied by men and never even apply.

Morale also suffers. When people are thwarted in their attempts to satisfy legitimate ambitions, discontent and frustration set in. Many women, unable to achieve their goals, have become bitter; they are hypercritical of men at higher levels, and spend their energies on voicing their criticism. When obvious cases of unfairness exist, it is also very easy for other women to blame their own failures on discrimination, instead of trying to improve their qualifications and demonstrate their capabilities.

We came across situations in several locations where whole departments had become demoralized as a result of one or two cases of apparent discrimination. When this happens, there can be little doubt that productivity suffers. We also heard first-hand stories of lack of cooperation, and even sabotage. In these circumstances, the Corporation is the loser right down the line.

RECOMMENDATIONS

There is no easy solution to the job access problem, for the context in which change must be effected is a complex one. The long-term answer certainly lies in changing attitudes, and that is bound to be a slow process. But the situation is such that the Corporation cannot afford to wait; behaviour must be altered in the immediate future, both in order to reduce discrimination in the selection of candidates, and to speed up the disappearance of the stereotype. Once women are seen to be able to do "men's jobs", the generalizations will start to lose their force.

The quickest remedy would, of course, be a coercive one: the introduction of special training and enforced quotas. The Task Force believes that such measures would be counterproductive; there would be instant resentment, and, if quotas were rigorously enforced, there might be cases where a woman got a job for which a male applicant was more highly qualified. A poorly qualified woman, given a job merely to satisfy the quota at a particular location, would do more harm than good to the cause of equal opportunity. Women, men, and the Corporation would suffer.

It must be recognized, too, that everything cannot be accomplished at once. No organization can absorb sweeping changes in the span of a few months. The mechanisms for change will need to fit into the CBC's overall human resources improvement program, as they are very closely related. Finally, even with total commitment to an equal opportunities program, we simply have not enough staff and resources to undertake all the necessary steps simultaneously.

With all this in mind, the Task Force recommends a 5-part program to ensure open access to all jobs, phased over a period of about 3 years (Figure 45). In the following pages each of the recommendations within the program is discussed in turn.

1. Develop and communicate throughout the Corporation an equal opportunity policy with detailed guidelines for its implementation.

As the very first step, we believe that the CBC should take a public and quite specific stance on equal opportunity. This would have three important results. First, it would make corporation policy absolutely clear to all employees, present and future; some people, including several supervisors and union officials, still believe that the CBC sanctions the idea of "jobs for men" and "jobs for women", despite the President's statement announcing the establishment of the Task Force. Second, it would provide a pattern for behaviour, by spelling out guidelines for the application of the policy. Third, it would lay the foundation for programs to reform employment and advancement practices. The policy and guidelines, which would be developed by the Office of Equal Opportunity recommended by the Task Force, should be as explicit as possible. They might well be adapted from the excellent federal Public Service guidelines, as indicated in Figure 46.

ACTION PROGRAM	TIMING		
	Year 1	Year 2	Year 3
PHASE I: MAKE UNMISTAKABLY CLEAR WHERE THE CBC STANDS	▬		
— Develop and communicate throughout the Corporation an explicit equal-opportunity policy with detailed guidelines for its application			
PHASE II: STRENGTHEN EMPLOYMENT AND ADVANCEMENT PROCESSES	▬▬		
Employment			
— Revise recruitment materials			
— Communicate equal opportunity policy to schools and other sources			
— Ensure that all external employment advertising invites both male and female applicants			
— Remove sex and marital status questions from application forms			
— Develop new interview guidelines			
Advancement			
— Post all jobs up to and including MSV			
— Establish consistent and prominent use of equal opportunity notice			
— Maintain inventory of women to be considered in certain selection decisions			
Both			
— Establish selection boards for all employment and advancement decisions for posted jobs			
PHASE III: DEVELOP AND IMPLEMENT TRAINING PROGRAMS TO CHANGE ATTITUDES	▬▬		
— Ensure that men/women awareness sessions are built into supervisory training program that is developed in 1975/76			
— Conduct pilot awareness sessions outside supervisory training, using professional resources			
PHASE IV: DEVELOP AND IMPLEMENT DETAILED AFFIRMATIVE ACTION PROGRAMS WITH WILLING LINE MANAGERS		▬▬	
— Develop programs to increase proportion of women in management and other key jobs through a combination of training and outside recruiting			
— Develop programs to break down sex stereotypes in lower level jobs through such means as recruiting, training, and temporary assignments		*Ongoing*	
PHASE V: KEEP MANAGEMENT AND EMPLOYEES INFORMED OF PROGRESS	▬▬		
— Monitor progress of major job-access measures and make semiannual reports to senior management			
— Publish annual report to staff on all aspects of progress on job-access programming			

Fig. 45   The Task Force recommends a 5-part program to improve job access

71

EQUAL CAREER OPPORTUNITY IN CBC*

POLICY STATEMENT

It is the policy of the CBC that decisions on both appointment and advancement in the Corporation must be based on the qualifications or suitability of a particular individual and not on the basis of characteristics assumed, accurately or inaccurately, to be associated with a particular category of people.

GUIDELINES FOR APPLICATION

1. Equal Opportunity Without
   Regard to Sex

To make an assumption about the capability or lack of capability of a particular individual solely on the basis of group tendencies is prejudice; to act on that assumption is discrimination. For example, the physical requirements of a job do not provide sufficient cause to limit that job to members of one sex. Instead the physical capacities of each individual must be taken into account. A job can be denied a particular individual if it can be shown that he or she is not physically capable of carrying out the duties of the position. Similarly, personal suitability is to be judged on a case-by-case basis, not on the basis of characteristics assumed to be associated with one sex.

The traditional sex-typing of a job as male or female is *not* sufficient reason to limit a position to members of one sex only. This means that the following factors are not, within themselves, sufficient grounds for offering appointments only to males or only to females:

- Strenuous or heavy physical labour
- Contact with the public or with particular groups
- Monotonous or routine duties
- Manual dexterity
- Travel to remote areas or travel with a person or persons of the opposite sex
- Geographic location
- Night work or shift work
- Working with teams or units of the opposite sex, whether as colleagues, subordinates, or superiors
- Limited advancement opportunities
- Exposure to weather
- Living or working facilities, or environment
- Isolation

* — *Adapted from the federal Public Service guidelines*

Fig. 46   The policy and guidelines should be as explicit as possible

In the areas of employment and advancement, a number of our recommendations should be easy to implement almost immediately. To begin with, the OEO should work with the Employment and Manpower Planning services to make their "mechanics" consistent with the equal opportunity policy. Specifically:

2. Revise all recruitment materials to eliminate sex stereotyping.

The brochures describing careers in the CBC should be revised immediately, and all old versions scrapped. New films that conform to the equal opportunity policy and do not perpetuate the stereotype should be prepared; in the meantime, the Wayne and Shuster film still in use by English Services should be withdrawn and placed in the Archives as a reminder of the past.

3. Communicate new equal opportunity policy to all major sources of outside candidates for employment.

Representatives of the Corporation should meet with officials of schools and placement bureaus to make clear the CBC's desire to break down sex stereotyping in all areas of work. The employment office should also circulate written materials, approved by the OEO, on the policy and its implications, to such sources of candidates.

The Task Force sees this initiative as only the first step in establishing a closer relationship between the Corporation and outside sources of candidates. For example, we believe that the CBC should make a concerted effort to see that all schools have the fullest possible information about CBC's future staff requirements as well as its equal opportunity policies.

4. Ensure that all external employment advertising invites both men and women applicants.

In order to ensure that external advertising also reflects the policy, all newspaper advertisements should carry a notice that the position is open to both men and women. These ads should go in the "neutral" section of the newspaper, or - if none exists - in both the "male" and "female" sections. CBC policy should be formally communicated to all media that carry such advertisements.

5. Work with unions to remove - where practical - sex from position titles.

While we are not anxious to burden the language with awkward words and phrases in order to make all titles clearly "sexless", we believe there are a number of cases where a simple change would remove any suggestion that jobs are for men or women only. "Cameraman", for instance, might become "camera operator".

6. **Revise application forms to remove questions on sex and marital status, and encourage use of initials rather than first names.**

Work should begin immediately on revision of application forms, to remove all questions on sex and marital status, and to encourage - through instructions on the form - the use of initials rather than given names.

7. **Redesign notice of vacancy form to include invitation to both men and women applicants.**

In the area of advancement, an immediate step should be taken; notice of vacancy forms, which are used to post jobs internally, should be redesigned to include a statement that the position being posted is open to both men and women.

8. **Develop new interview guidelines and circulate to all employment personnel and supervisors.**

Also in the short term, the OEO should develop new interview guidelines. A short memorandum should be circulated to all employment personnel and supervisors emphasizing that relevant information should be elicited by asking professional rather than personal questions - for example: *"Are you free to travel?"*, not *"Are you married?"*. This kind of example should be included in the memorandum. It should be made clear that adherence to these guidelines is mandatory, whether for employment or advancement interviews.

While we believe that these simple but visible changes would in themselves have some impact, we do not believe that they are sufficient to solve the problem of job access. We also recommend three administrative changes, designed to ensure that women are not excluded from the advancement process.

9. **Post all jobs up to and including MS V.**

We are aware that there is considerable reluctance on the part of many managers to extend the posting procedure beyond the present limits required by union contract. However, there was an overwhelming demand for such an extension among the employees we met. Women believe it would give them a better chance of at least being considered for positions that are traditionally filled by men; and men too feel that it will give them greater visibility and opportunity.

Extension of the posting system would result in more applications for these jobs and thus create an additional burden for management people who are already extremely busy. However, we believe that choosing the right people for management jobs at the lower and middle levels is so important that this consideration outweighs any other.

There is some danger that the posting of all jobs up to and including the MS V level may simply increase frustration by raising the hopes of unqualified employees. To reduce the chances of this happening, we believe the first step should be to explain the purpose of the expansion; the second, to define more rigorously on the notice of vacancy the nature of the job functions and the requisite qualifications. On balance, we are convinced that the benefits to be gained by expansion of the posting procedure would outweigh any burdens it might bring. Women will be more visible as candidates for middle management jobs, and the change will be seen as a progressive step by both women and men.

But - possibly because of past rebuffs - some talented women may still not apply for jobs they are qualified to fill. And they will often be unaware of vacancies above MS V. The Task Force therefore recommends that the Corporation:

10. Have manpower planning personnel, working with the Office of Equal Opportunity, develop an inventory of women, to be consulted by decision makers.

The Corporation's manpower planning personnel are currently building up a data bank, with information on the qualifications, work experience, and aspirations of employees. The data bank is being compiled through the use of questionnaires. The inventory of women (Figure 47) should build upon this framework; OEO personnel would encourage women who have not yet completed the questionnaire to do so - and would, it is expected, work with the Manpower office to remove those questions to which women who have already completed it have taken exception. It would thereafter be up to the Manpower Planning or Personnel office to maintain the lists.

Each time a vacancy occurs in a position where women are not yet proportionately represented, for example, in management or TV production, the inventory should be made available to the supervisors concerned. They would then be able to encourage suitably qualified women to apply.

Once these mechanisms have been established, many more qualified women will be brought to the attention of the decision makers. But, until the new systems are in place, how can the CBC be sure they will get an even break? There is much evidence that conscious and unconscious discrimination does take place; since such discrimination is based on attitudes that die hard, it is not realistic to suppose that all supervisors will immediately conform to the Corporation's standards of equality if the decisions are theirs alone. This fact is emphasized by the overwhelming demand among the employees, male as well as female, whom we interviewed, for the consistent use of selection boards. The Task Force therefore recommends that the CBC:

11. Establish selection boards for all vacancies from above lowest entry level up to and including MS V.

Selection boards, if properly constituted, are one way of preventing jobs from being filled - or "promised" - before they are posted. Their use would

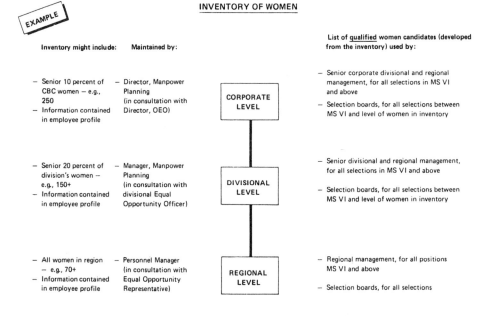

INVENTORY OF WOMEN

EXAMPLE

Inventory might include:	Maintained by:		List of <u>qualified</u> women candidates (developed from the inventory) used by:
– Senior 10 percent of CBC women – e.g., 250 – Information contained in employee profile	– Director, Manpower Planning (in consultation with Director, OEO)	CORPORATE LEVEL	– Senior corporate divisional and regional management, for all selections in MS VI and above – Selection boards, for all selections between MS VI and level of women in inventory
– Senior 20 percent of division's women – e.g., 150+ – Information contained in employee profile	– Manager, Manpower Planning (in consultation with divisional Equal Opportunity Officer)	DIVISIONAL LEVEL	– Senior divisional and regional management, for all selections in MS VI and above – Selection boards, for all selections between MS VI and level of women in inventory
– All women in region – e.g., 70+ – Information contained in employee profile	– Personnel Manager (in consultation with Equal Opportunity Representative)	REGIONAL LEVEL	– Regional management, for all positions MS VI and above – Selection boards, for all selections

* – *Building on work already done with employee profiles*

Fig. 47   *An inventory of women should be developed and used by decision makers*

76

help to reduce discrimination and favouritism of all kinds; and they would bring the Personnel office back into the employment picture, and give it a more effective role.

To function properly, the boards would have to work systematically and include the right people, who would have to understand their roles clearly. A summary table showing the suggested composition of selection boards, the roles of each participant, and the functioning of the boards, is given in Figure 48.

In recommending the use of selection boards up to and including MS V, we feel that the drawbacks are outweighed by the benefits. Selection boards will, of course, make more administrative work; and by increasing the number of people involved, more valuable time is spent in coming to a decision. Confidentiality might be more difficult to maintain; and the supervisor's authority might seem to be in question. On the other hand, time and effort spent to bring about a significant reduction in cases of discrimination against women, and to improve personnel choices generally, are well worth the cost. And the consistent use of this system would do a great deal to restore the staff's faith in the fairness and wisdom of the Corporation's decisions.

The recommendations so far with respect to job access have had to do with stating and communicating equal opportunity policies and guidelines for their application, and with mechanisms to ensure that women are seriously considered for all jobs for which they are qualified. Successful implementation of this program will go far to change the atmosphere in which women find themselves in the CBC, and ought, over a period of time, to break down the barriers to full access to jobs.

But, as we said at the beginning of this section, policies and guidelines aim primarily at changing behaviour in the short term, rather than at changing attitudes. The Task Force believes that an immediate attack on the attitudinal front is needed as well, and we believe that the most effective approach is through training. We therefore have two recommendations with respect to training, one concerned with supervisors, and the other with staff generally:

12. Ensure that awareness sessions are built into the supervisory training program that is being developed in 1975/76.

Outside the CBC, materials have been professionally developed to help men and women understand the problems of working as equal colleagues; for example, they help people to see the dangers in acting on stereotypes of groups of people, and to learn to understand the differences in emotional reactions. Sessions making use of these materials should therefore be an integral part of the supervisory training program to be developed in 1975/76 as part of the CBC's program to improve its management of human resources.

COMPOSITION	ROLES	FUNCTIONING
Board should number three to five, and always include: — The supervisor — Employment officer (or other representative of Manpower Planning Office) — Recent or current occupant of same or similar job For lower level jobs, these three are sufficient provided: — At least one is an objective (unprejudiced) woman, or an objective (unprejudiced) man For higher level jobs, these three and: — Another supervisor in related department — At supervisor's discretion, his/her supervisor For "sex stereotyped" (e.g., over 90 percent of one sex) jobs, where there are both male and female candidates, these three and: — Representative of OEO	Of Supervisor: — Make final decision Of Employment Officer: — Prescreen candidates and inform those who are unqualified — Assist supervisor in selection of board members — Present board member with prior information on candidates and job requirements — Set time and place of meeting — In absence of OEO representative, remind board of equal opportunity policy and interview guidelines — Follow up with candidates Of OEO Representative: — Bring to board's attention equal opportunity policy and interview guidelines — Monitor questioning of candidates — Take up, subsequently, with any individual evidencing prejudice, the nature and seriousness of his or her bias	Before Interviews: — Review job specifications and qualifications of remaining candidates — Discuss demands of position with supervisor During Interviews: — Follow interview guidelines developed by employment personnel and OEO After Interviews: — Rate candidates individually — Compare and discuss ratings — Work for consensus — Give supervisor time for reflection, if he or she disagrees — Document rationale for decision in writing — Decide how candidates should be given feedback

Fig. 48   To be effective, selection boards must be properly constituted, and members should fully understand their role and functions

13. Conduct pilot awareness sessions outside supervisory training, using professional resources; extend these sessions across the CBC if they are successful.

A number of organizations, including a major U.S. broadcasting system, have hired professionals to conduct awareness sessions for large numbers of personnel at all levels, and consider that these programs have been successful in breaking down sex stereotypes. The CBC should begin by carrying out a pilot session, under the leadership of the Director of the OEO, working with corporate and divisional training personnel. If the pilot session is successful, similar programs should be carried out at all locations.

Up to this point, we have recommended policies and actions to be put into effect throughout the Corporation. In many cases, however, the best way of achieving results will be by action at the local level. It is important, therefore, that when senior managers at a particular location are really eager to promote equality of opportunity, mechanisms exist to help them to do so, in a manner that is both realistic and acceptable to all the people concerned. It is likely that affirmative action at individual centres might be of two kinds, both of which are briefly discussed below.

The first kind of affirmative action program would be aimed at increasing the number of women in management and other key jobs, in order to redress the balance between men's and women's share of the corporate wealth; to provide models of success for other women; and to accelerate changes in the attitudes of men. A location undertaking this kind of program would start by identifying specific job vacancies that were likely to occur in the areas or departments concerned - management, production, etc. There would then be a search for female candidates, inside and if necessary outside the CBC, who seemed to have the potential for the work concerned. They would then receive any special training required, so that they would be fully qualified to compete for the position when it became available. This might require job rotation or courses in management and leadership. Should a woman eventually be selected to fill the vacancy, it might also be necessary to prepare her new coworkers, either by means of a training seminar or by individual discussions. There should also be provision to give her guidance and support, once she is established in the job.

The second kind of affirmative action program, designed to break down sex stereotyping in less senior positions, might take a number of forms. It should be remembered that the intent is to open all job categories to both women and men; some men have as we mentioned earlier, been refused jobs as script assistants, on the basis that *"this is a girl's job"*. From the point of view of the Corporation, open access presents a wider pool of recruits for all functions, and enables the CBC to make better use of all its people.

To set in motion a program to desegregate jobs, it would first be necessary for local managers, in consultation with a representative of the OEO, the local Women's Association, and such other interested groups as unions, to identify the job categories where the employees and the CBC would most benefit from integration. Next, specific barriers to integrating these jobs would have to be determined. For example, job specifications would be examined to see whether they contain requirements that discourage one or other sex, and whether such requirements are really relevant. For certain jobs, the barrier might of course be lack of skills; if such skills could be acquired through training courses of fairly brief duration, this obstacle might be overcome. And local management could consider paying all of the tuition fees for an individual's outside course, rather than 50 percent, if he or she is gaining qualifications for a position traditionally held by the opposite sex. Finally, an overall plan of action would have to be mapped out, taking the difficulties into account. A representative of the OEO would work with the locations' line managers and the unions concerned to end segregation in the chosen category.

Two examples illustrate the kind of project that might be undertaken. A logical place to start would be at the entry level. Very few women are hired as office juniors - a job that often leads, as we have pointed out before, to careers in accounting or film editing. Many locations do not consider hiring women as office juniors because it is assumed that *"girls can't carry those heavy mailbags"*. Other locations have specialized the work of the mailroom staffs so that only one or two people are required to do "porter" duty. A location consciously trying to desegregate might find that it is possible to hire more women in this area by arranging the work of the department differently. Subsequently, the supervisor should see that men and women have the same opportunities to advance. Simultaneously, the location might launch a recruitment program to encourage men to become stenographers and secretaries.

A somewhat more ambitious program might be aimed at breaking down the sex stereotyping of television script and production assistant positions. One way to accomplish this is to seek men as candidates for script assistant vacancies, and women for production assistant vacancies. But this would be a slow process, and a location might decide to merge the two positions on a trial basis - with, of course, the understanding that the local union would have to be in sympathy with the idea and prepared to cooperate. The local union would have to work with its national executive, local management, and a representative of the OEO to help plan the project. Such a program might involve either a few script and production assistants, who would trade functions for a time, or it might involve the whole group. Joint training programs might well be required, and it would be necessary to design an orderly system of measuring the success of the program.

We believe that specific programs such as this, if they are properly set up and explained to the staff, would speed progress in an area where changes do not come easily, despite goodwill and clear policies. The Task Force therefore recommends that the Corporation:

14. **Develop and implement affirmative action programs to increase the proportion of women in management and other key jobs, and to break down segregation by sex in positions at lower levels.**

These programs should use recruiting, formal training, job rotation, restructuring of some positions, and other means in a coordinated effort to achieve a realistic and specific result (e.g., "two female office juniors by the end of 1975 in our location").

15. Carry out the action programs on a decentralized basis, working with senior managers.

The Office of Equal Opportunity would encourage senior line managers at all levels and locations to develop action programs, and would provide advice and assistance in their execution, working also with the appropriate human resources managers (training, compensation, and so on), unions, and women's associations.

We have tried in this chapter to attack from several angles the problem of women's lack of access to the majority of jobs in the CBC. Up to this point, we have recommended policies and procedures to improve the selection process both in hiring and in transfers and promotions; the use of training in the difficult process of effecting changes in attitudes; and the setting up of action programs to redress the imbalance in the share of corporate wealth, to provide "models", and to break down segregation at all levels. Before leaving this, the most important and challenging of all the problem areas, we have two more recommendations which we believe are essential to the coordination and success of the others:

16. Monitor, through the Office of Equal Opportunity, progress both in the Corporation as a whole, and in individual locations.

The OEO would keep a continuing record of such important facts as the percentage of women in management and other key positions, as well as of the degree of integration in job functions that have, until now, been segregated by sex. It would also keep a close eye on trends in employment and advancement.

17. Present, through the Office of Equal Opportunity, regular reports to management on the progress - or lack of progress - in the matter of job access in the Corporation as a whole and in individual locations; and issue an annual report to all employees.

It is essential that the Corporation's concern with attaining equality of opportunity for all its employees should remain a live issue, and that both management and staff be reminded on a regular basis of this concern. While we would expect the OEO to make full use of CLOSED CIRCUIT and other informal means of communication with staff, we believe that regular factual reports are a necessity.

We have discussed at great length the problem of job access, since it clearly affects the greatest numbers of women in the CBC. We repeat that this is not a problem with any simple solutions, nor is it one that will disappear in a few months. We believe, however, that, if acted upon, our 17 recommendations will go a long way to alleviate the situation, over the course of the next 3 years.

In the next chapter, we deal with problems that also result, to a large extent, from people's attitudes - the problems of secretaries.

* * * * *

MANAGEMENT RESPONSE

Of the 17 recommendations on job access made by the Task Force, management accepts 14 in full just as they are described earlier in this chapter. The other 3 recommendations are accepted in direction and principle, but have several qualifications as to details - all of which will be described below. Equally important, we would stress that the Task Force has concluded that 3 years will be required for full implementation.

1. **Develop and communicate throughout the Corporation an equal opportunity policy with detailed guidelines for its implementation.**
   Accepted in full.

2. **Revise all recruitment materials to eliminate sex stereotyping.**

   Accepted in full.

3. **Communicate new equal opportunity policy to all major sources of outside candidates for employment.**
   Accepted in full.

4. **Ensure that all external employment advertising invites both men and women applicants.**
   Accepted in full.

5. **Work with unions to remove - where practical - sex from position titles.**
   Accepted in full.

6. **Revise application forms to remove questions on sex and marital status, and encourage use of initials rather than first names.**
   Accepted in part. As we understand it, the intent of this recommendation is to encourage employment personnel and supervisors to process further all outside candidates whose application forms indicate they are qualified on

82

paper for a particular job, and to make it more difficult, if not impossible, to exclude at the application stage anyone from consideration on the basis of sex and marital status. With this intent we agree fully. However, we have two problems with the details of the portion of the recommendation that relates to sex (i.e., *"remove questions on sex . . . and encourage use of initials rather than first names"*).

First, there is the practical problem of identifying the literally thousands of applicants the Corporation must process each year. Specifically, because of the large numbers of Smiths, Tremblays, etc. who apply, first names and sex are often essential to determine who is who! Second, and equally important, we feel that the other recommendations of the Task Force attack the problem in a more direct and positive way. For example, the recommended policy and guidelines on equal opportunity will make very clear that candidates are not to be excluded on the basis of sex, and employment personnel will have a clear mandate to ensure that they are observed. Withholding information on sex would, in our view, create administrative difficulties without helping solve the problem it is meant to attack.

As for eliminating marital status from the initial application form, for much the same reasons we feel that there is little to be gained. However, since there would be no administrative problems incurred in doing so, we are willing to rely on the Task Force's judgment that the gains, however small, would be worthwhile. In net, therefore, we concur with removing questions on marital status from applications, but must disagree with excluding queries on sex and with encouraging the use of initials rather than first names.

7. **Redesign notice of vacancy form to include invitation to both men and women applicants.**
   Accepted in full.

8. **Develop new interview guidelines and circulate to all employment personnel and supervisors.**
   Accepted in full.

9. **Post all jobs up to and including MS V.**
   Accepted in full. Management agrees with the Task Force's conclusion that the many potential problems in expanding job postings *(a)* can be minimized by such steps as carefully communicating the purpose of expanded postings, and more rigorously defining qualifications of the position to be filled and *(b)* in any event, are outweighed by the benefits of greater visibility and opportunity for women *and* men.

We would stress, however, the Task Force's conclusion that this will not be implemented immediately across the country. Rather, the group does not expect complete implementation until a year to a year and one-half into the equal opportunity program, because of the work required to set up a truly effective posting process.

10. Have manpower planning personnel, working with the Office of Equal Opportunity, develop an inventory of women, to be consulted by decision makers.
Accepted in full. We believe this to be a key recommendation in ensuring that women are systematically considered for all vacancies. However, we would re-emphasize the Task Force's points that *(a)* the purpose of the list is not to force the decision maker to accept a woman, but rather to make him or her fully aware of any qualified female candidates that may exist and *(b)* for a particular vacancy, a list of qualified male candidates should obviously be developed as well.

11. Establish selection boards for all vacancies from above lowest entry level up to and including MS V.
Accepted, but subject to subsequent approval of the details and timing of implementation. In management's view, this essential recommendation will be very difficult and time-consuming to implement effectively. For example, our experience in several locations with the selection board process indicates the necessity of careful prescreening to eliminate clearly unqualified applicants, fully briefed and skillful board members, well-structured interview questions, and thorough follow-up procedures that are well executed. Meeting these requirements is clearly a tough job, particularly because selection board members have full-time positions in the organization and are able to participate on boards only in a few hours "stolen" for them. For these and related reasons, then, we accept in full the Task Force's recommendation to establish selection boards, but we wish to approve subsequently the details of implementation to ensure that the process is thoroughly and professionally conceived.

12. Ensure that awareness sessions are built into the supervisory training program that is being developed in 1975/76.
Accepted in full.

13. Conduct pilot awareness sessions outside supervisory training, using professional resources; extend these sessions across the CBC if they are successful.
Accepted in full.

14. **Develop and implement affirmative action programs to increase the proportion of women in management and other key jobs, and to break down segregation by sex in positions at lower levels.**
Accepted in full.

15. **Carry out the action programs on a decentralized basis, working with senior managers.**
Accepted in full.

16. **Monitor, through the Office of Equal Opportunity, progress both in the Corporation as a whole, and in individual locations.**
Accepted in full.

17. **Present, through the Office of Equal Opportunity, regular reports to management on the progress - or lack of progress - in the matter of job access in the Corporation as a whole and in individual locations; and issue an annual report to all employees.**
Accepted in full. As we understand it, the Task Force's intent is that employees receive at least annually all the facts they need to judge the progress of the program; with this we fully agree. However, while the facts should be communicated in writing, we do not believe that an alaborate "annual report" - in the sense that term is generally used - will be required.

4. SECRETARIES

The secretary's job is the only one that the Task Force singled out for separate treatment. This was not our original intention, but we quickly found that there were good reasons to do so.

First of all, secretaries are clearly the most discontented group in the Corporation. Turnover of secretaries in the Corporation is much higher than that of any other group of employees (Figure 49 and see Figure 34). And interviews and written submissions included the following comments, each of which was echoed, often in almost the same words, right across the country:

> *"I have been a secretary for 6 years; whether you are a script assistant, a secretary in the costumes department, archives, or management, the problem remains the same:* servir ces grands seigneurs! . . . *"; "I'm watched over like a 3-year-old . . . "; "Men keep you from being promoted if you're clever; he needs you to strengthen* his *position . . . "; "Secretaries' jobs are regarded as very poor; you're only a secretary, is the attitude, and they make you feel you are nothing . . . "; "Secretaries within the CBC are not given the status and salary scale they deserve in comparison with other positions in the Corporation . . . "; "You're branded: Once a secretary, always a secretary . . . "; "What started as a simple courtesy becomes a duty: cigarettes, concert tickets, the bank, etc.; the ways to protest are not always the best: absenteeism, indifference to the work . . . ".*

These comments give the flavour of the frustration we found to be so prevalent among secretaries. Such discontent is a serious matter, not only because one-fifth of all women on staff are secretaries (Figure 50), but also because their work is vital to the running of the Corporation. They carry out a high proportion of the work load of many departments. Many of them provide continuity of operation when their supervisors are absent. They are the "voice of the department" in dealing with other departments, and the "voice of the CBC" in handling calls and greeting visitors from outside the organization. They are, in short, important both to the CBC's internal functioning and to its outward image. Moreover, a very large number of women get their first impressions of the CBC from the vantage point of the secretarial function. Of all the women hired in 1973, 41 percent began in secretarial or stenographic jobs (Figure 51).

We have already mentioned the high rate of turnover that results from the discontent. But among those that do remain on the job, there can be little doubt that in many cases they lose pride in their work. The Corporation as well as the women suffer as a result.

86

TURNOVER RATES OF CBC WOMEN

(percentage — 1973)

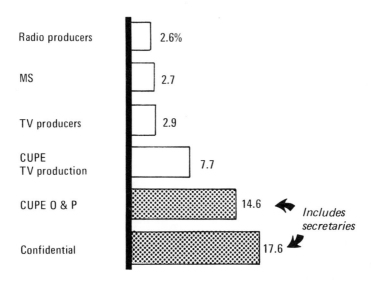

Fig. 49 Turnover of secretaries is much higher than of any other group of female employees

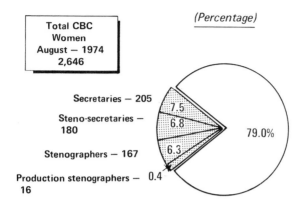

(Percentage)

Total CBC
Women
August — 1974
2,646

Secretaries — 205

Steno-secretaries —
180

Stenographers — 167

Production stenographers —
16

7.5
6.8
6.3
0.4
79.0%

Fig. 50   One-fifth of CBC women are secretaries

STARTING POSITIONS FOR WOMEN HIRED IN 1973*
(percentage)

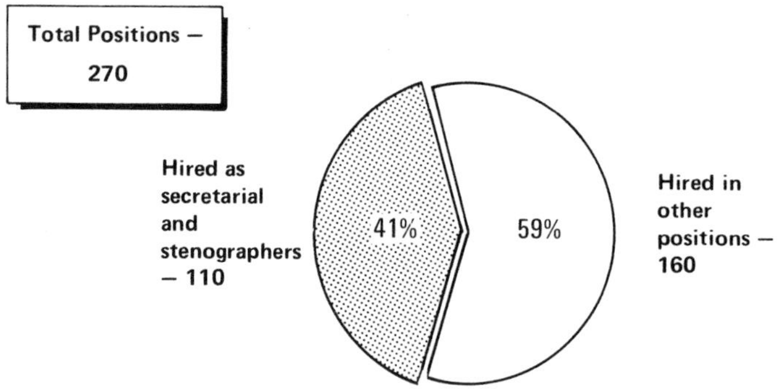

Total Positions —
270

Hired as
secretarial
and
stenographers
— 110

41%

59%

Hired in
other
positions —
160

* — In 11 largest CBC locations

Fig. 51   Almost half of the women hired from outside join the CBC as secretaries

88

Because of the degree of discontent, it appeared to the Task Force that there must be something wrong with the job itself. So we set out to analyze it, and to see if the specific complaints fell into patterns.

We concluded that the nature of the secretarial position would cause problems regardless of the sex of the people involved, because the job is an extension of someone else's, rather than an entity in itself; if there were no boss, there would be no secretary. This single fact leads to a whole series of related problems (Figure 52). For example, secretaries' responsibilities are ill defined, and vary considerably according to the style and work habits of the individual boss. And secretaries are totally dependent on one person's evaluation of their performance. What is more, their salary depends entirely on how highly paid a secretary the boss is entitled to by reason of rank.

When secretaries look for promotion, they see no logical career paths except within the secretarial function itself - whereas for other entry-level positions, such as the office junior, various routes are open. In smaller centres, even the secretarial career ladder is very limited; positions at other centres are not posted nationally, and if a secretary did succeed in getting a transfer so as to take an advancement elsewhere, moving expenses would not be paid.

Career problems also arise out of the highly personalized nature of the working relationship, which makes many secretaries feel that they work only for a particular person, and not for the Corporation. In some cases, the boss makes it clear that any attempt by a secretary to get a promotion would be viewed as disloyalty. It is true that other people, such as administrative assistants, also have jobs that are to a point "extensions" of the boss's job; but the secretary too often finds that the boss unloads only the minor tasks and menial chores, without delegating any responsibilities. When errands unrelated to CBC work, such as picking up laundry or typing personal cheques, are added, the relationship begins to resemble that of master and servant. As a result, secretaries may become "only" secretaries in their own eyes and in the eyes of others. It takes rare dedication at this stage not to lose pride in one's work, and not to retaliate in small ways.

So the nature of the job itself carries the seeds of discontent, regardless of the sexes of secretary and boss. But when over 90 percent of the bosses are men, and 99.5 percent of the stenographers and secretaries are women, another element is added. Indeed, comments made repeatedly to the Task Force by men across the country show that they do not take "the girls" and their work too seriously:

> "Well, a nice looking secretary is an asset to the office . . . ";
> "Men wouldn't make good secretaries, because there's not
> enough challenge; you have to have a special inner feeling
> about challenge; women in their nature don't have this . . .";
> "We have higher expectations of men - a man would look
> silly as a secretary . . . ;" "Women make better secretaries;
> they have quick hands for typing, and a tolerance for
> detail . . . "; "I don't mind asking a woman to clear off my
> desk and get coffee, but I wouldn't feel right asking that of a
> man . . . "; "Everyone would think I was a homosexual if I

89

JOB CONCEPT

NEGATIVE CONSEQUENCES

OVERALL EFFECT

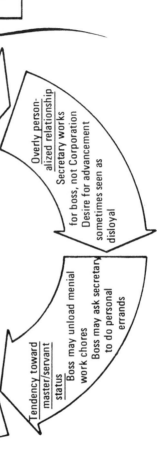

Devaluation of function
- Others may perceive secretaries as unimportant
- Secretaries may lose pride in work

Unclear career paths
- Logical career progression not apparent
- Advancement may depend on boss' success

Overly personalized relationship
- Secretary works for boss, not Corporation
- Desire for advancement sometimes seen as disloyal

Compensation unrelated to duties
- Salary levels tied to boss ranking

Tendency toward master/servant status
- Boss may unload menial work chores
- Boss may ask secretary to do personal errands

Ill-defined responsibility
- Duties and work load vary with style and work habits of boss
- Criteria for performance are fuzzy
- Secretary totally dependent on boss' evaluation

Extension of someone else, rather than free-standing entity
- "Generally performs routine clerical functions to relieve executive officer of minor tasks"

Fig. 52   The nature of the secretarial position leads to problems, regardless of sex

90

had a male secretary . . . "; "Me - a secretary? No bloody
way I'd get a cup of coffee for a guy . . . "; "A boss-secretary
relationship is like father and daughter . . . "; "A man
couldn't live on a secretary's salary . . . "; "Stenos are a dime
a dozen . . . ".

The sex stereotype is thus carried to its extreme in the way many men regard secretaries. And so the problems inherent in the job are compounded by the attitudes towards secretaries and their work expressed by the men around them. The three most important aspects of work that are affected are advancement, compensation, and treatment on the job. Our findings in each of these areas are given in the following pages.

ADVANCEMENT

Secretaries generally look for advancement in one of three major functions. Some - although their number is diminishing - would like to make their careers as secretaries. Many others, seeing this as a "helping" rather than a "doing" role, look elsewhere; in the CBC, mainly towards administration and production.

For those who intend to continue in the secretarial line, a career path does exist in the larger centres. Figure 53 demonstrates the path, through an analysis of age groups, years of service, and salary levels. And 1973 figures from across the country suggest that secretaries move along that path at a fairly rapid rate (Figure 54). Any generalization to the effect that most bosses selfishly prevent their secretaries from advancing, or that secretaries cannot get promotions unless their bosses are upgraded, is therefore probably untrue.

However, on an individual basis, the prospects may not be so encouraging. The career opportunities in the smaller centres are limited, because there are relatively few senior secretarial positions; and a significant number of qualified women probably are held back for the wrong reasons; bosses have been known to discourage other supervisors from "stealing" people from their departments.

Many secretaries who do not wish to remain within the secretarial function would like to move into jobs in administration, in one of the office services departments, for example. Their education often points in this direction, and frequently their experience has made them thoroughly familiar with office operations. But there seem to be obstacles in the way of this route too, of which the principal one is simply the lack of established career paths. Supervisors' attitudes may also set up barriers, either from selfish motives *("I need her here")* or because the supervisor puts no value on secretarial experience. In the words of one supervisor - *"She couldn't take on a job that requires her to operate independently".*

But the career that seems most attractive to those secretaries who wish to move into a different area is one in program production. Many women have accepted secretarial jobs because this seemed to be the only door open to

APPARENT SECRETARIAL PATH
TOTAL CBC*

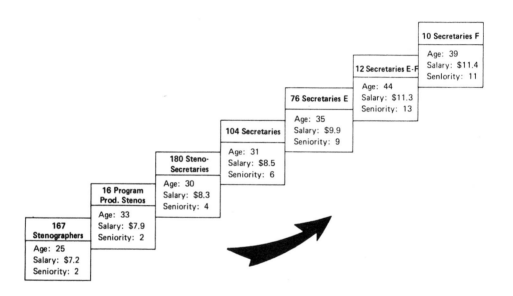

167 Stenographers
Age: 25
Salary: $7.2
Seniority: 2

16 Program Prod. Stenos
Age: 33
Salary: $7.9
Seniority: 2

180 Steno-Secretaries
Age: 30
Salary: $8.3
Seniority: 4

104 Secretaries
Age: 31
Salary: $8.5
Seniority: 6

76 Secretaries E
Age: 35
Salary: $9.9
Seniority: 9

12 Secretaries E-F
Age: 44
Salary: $11.3
Seniority: 13

10 Secretaries F
Age: 39
Salary: $11.4
Senlority: 11

* — *All data are averages*

Fig. 53 Across the CBC, a secretarial career path does exist

1973 ADVANCEMENTS IN LARGEST CENTRES
(Percentage of people in category who received advancements)

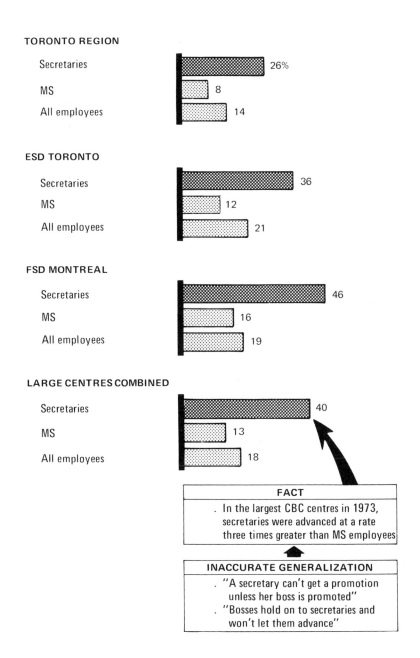

TORONTO REGION

Secretaries   26%

MS   8

All employees   14

ESD TORONTO

Secretaries   36

MS   12

All employees   21

FSD MONTREAL

Secretaries   46

MS   16

All employees   19

LARGE CENTRES COMBINED

Secretaries   40

MS   13

All employees   18

FACT

. In the largest CBC centres in 1973, secretaries were advanced at a rate three times greater than MS employees

INACCURATE GENERALIZATION

. "A secretary can't get a promotion unless her boss is promoted"
. "Bosses hold on to secretaries and won't let them advance"

Fig. 54 In comparison to management and employees generally, secretaries seem to progress quite rapidly along the career path

them, and have then become frustrated at finding the position such a poor starting point for a career in programming. To begin with, openings are few in "women's jobs" such as TV script assistant and radio program or production assistant, and the turnover in these jobs is low. Recently, in one large network centre, there were more than 80 applicants (mostly secretaries) for one position as script assistant.

Secretaries believe that they get less than full consideration for those production openings that do occur. A lot of frustration arises because the secretaries concerned may be unfamiliar with the workings of the program departments; this feeling is particularly strong at Engineering Headquarters and Head Office, where many of the women on staff have never seen a studio. Finally, in many cases they feel there is little point in applying at all, since decisions appear to have been made before the job is posted.

Of course, it is true that some secretaries, like other personnel, are simply not qualified for the job they may want in administration or production. But for those who are qualified, the barriers are real. Attitudes to the secretary's role and lack of career paths are the main obstacles; and removing them is not an easy undertaking.

How, then, can CBC make a realistic start? The experience of other organizations in handling similar problems provides some useful pointers. Some firms have adopted a completely different concept of the secretary's role and career. They see the secretary as part of the general administrative organization, on assignment to her boss - much as the script assistant is assigned. Under this arrangement, the secretary has recourse to her own supervisor, as well as to her current boss. She is assigned to duties for which she is qualified, with opportunities for more responsibility if she adds to her skills. She has a specific job description, and is paid on the basis of an evaluation of the position. Figure 55 shows how the system also builds in career paths. This approach, if properly handled, can allow secretaries to become familiar with several departments.

An organization closer in purpose and structure to our own has worked out a different solution to the problem. CBS restructures jobs on a continuing basis, depending on the individual occupying the position, and the needs of the department. Three main steps are taken:

1. Managers are asked to identify problems: a highly qualified secretary may be blocked from advancement, for instance, or a secretary may be performing administrative duties for which she is not receiving recognition.

2. The department affected is evaluated with regard to its objectives, activities, and individuals' talents.

3. An action plan is developed and implemented that may include restructuring job responsibilities, changing salary classifications accordingly, and moving people as necessary, either inside or outside the department.

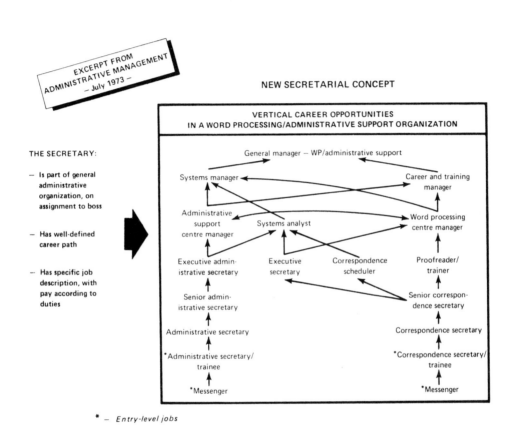

NEW SECRETARIAL CONCEPT

VERTICAL CAREER OPPORTUNITIES IN A WORD PROCESSING/ADMINISTRATIVE SUPPORT ORGANIZATION

THE SECRETARY:

— Is part of general administrative organization, on assignment to boss

— Has well-defined career path

— Has specific job description, with pay according to duties

General manager — WP/administrative support

Systems manager

Career and training manager

Administrative support centre manager

Systems analyst

Word processing centre manager

Executive administrative secretary

Executive secretary

Correspondence scheduler

Proofreader/ trainer

Senior administrative secretary

Senior correspondence secretary

Administrative secretary

Correspondence secretary

*Administrative secretary/ trainee

*Correspondence secretary/ trainee

*Messenger

*Messenger

* — Entry-level jobs

Fig. 55   One new secretarial career concept involves integration into a word processing/administrative organization

95

This quite flexible method has apparently met with a good deal of success, and network authorities hope soon to have very few purely secretarial positions. Management also feels that it is both making better use of the secretaries on staff, and succeeding in recruiting people with real potential.

The time and resources available did not permit the Task Force to reach a firm conclusion about the exact nature of the system that would work best for the CBC. Recognizing the need for further work in this area, our recommendations related to advancement for secretaries are that the Corporation:

> **18. Establish an action program that gives special encouragement to qualified secretaries to advance into administration and production.**

> **19. Undertake, as a first step, a project in an English Services region outside Toronto to design and implement new advancement paths.**

An English Services region outside Toronto is suggested, since we believe that projects resulting from the Task Force's recommendations should be spread across the country, not carried out entirely in the network centres. The centre chosen should be large enough to include a number of secretaries in both program and other departments. The team conducting the project would be under the direction of the Office of Equal Opportunity, and should include representatives of the secretarial group involved, the local or regional personnel office, and CUPE (Office and Professional).

The project team would be expected to do five things. First, it would list the possible approaches to developing advancement paths for secretaries, drawing upon the experience of other companies and of the Public Service. Possible approaches might include restructuring of individual jobs to help the occupant to specialize or learn new skills, or experimenting with a separate "administrative services" organization, or both. Second, the team would evaluate the chances of success of each approach, pointing out the practical implications, and recommend procedures that might be applied in other locations. Third, it would put the full program into practice in the centre chosen; fourth, based on the outcome of the pilot program, it would be able to recommend an overall CBC policy and a Canada-wide implementation program.

The fifth and final task of the project team would be to review the status of the secretaries classified as "confidential", recommending any changes that seemed necessary. We singled out the confidential secretaries because women in most locations believe this group has special problems. They point out that confidentials have no recourse to a union, yet are clearly not part of management. *"We're looked on as management finks"*, one said, *"but actually no one tells us anything"*. Many of them believe - probably wrongly in most cases - that they lose out financially; while they recognize the benefits (they are paid from 1 to 6 percent more than union employees at the same level), they point to the lower overtime rates, and the lower minimum credit for weekend work. And a number question whether the Industrial Disputes and Investigations Act, which defines confidential status, is uniformly and properly applied.

COMPENSATION

Next to chances for advancement, the hottest issue among secretaries is "rug ranking" - a term that probably originated within the Public Service, where, traditionally, as a boss climbed the departmental ladder, he was entitled not only to a more luxurious carpet, but also to a better paid secretary (Figure 56). In other words, the secretary's salary increased at the same rate as the size of the rug - hence, rug ranked.

The CBC, and indeed most industrial corporations (Figure 57), has been using this formula for some years. There is something to be said for it from the Corporation's point of view; it is realistic in its assumption that the secretary's job is, at present, an extension of her boss's job; so the importance of his work will to some extent determine the importance of hers. For example, it is assumed that the higher his management level, the greater her responsibilities, and the more embarrassing and costly a mistake on her part would be. And, of course, the system is easy to administer, since job evaluation is not required, the secretary's salary being determined solely by the level of the boss she works for (Figure 58).

But the fact that the system is in common use and is easy to administer does not mean it is good. In practice, among CBC women it causes considerable resentment, which appears to be justified. For one thing, the CBC secretary's work often does not depend on the boss's level; she may be given more responsibility than the secretary of her boss's boss. Or she may actually work for several people, and in doing so have to satisfy often conflicting demands. Second, without an evaluation system similar to that used for *all other jobs in the Corporation* (Figure 59), objective comparison with other secretarial positions is impossible. As a result, many secretaries believe their work is undervalued. Finally, in the absence of any proper evaluation system, the secretary's feeling of dependency on the person she works for is reinforced.

On the grounds of that dependency alone, the Royal Commission on the Status of Women recommended the abolition of rug ranking in the federal Public Service 4 years ago (Figure 60). The Public Service has had the matter under consideration for some time, and finally, after over a year of intensive study, it will adopt a new evaluation system for its 6,000 secretaries in April 1975 (Figure 61). The new system is expected to have several major advantages. Because job descriptions will be much more precise, it will be possible to hire people whose skills better fit the particular job to be filled. It will provide a basis for a more realistic evaluation of an individual's performance. The analysis of its own functioning that each department will have to carry out to develop the necessary job descriptions will be useful both to the individual departments and to the Personnel office. The morale of women in the Public Service is expected to improve greatly. And finally, it will mean the end of an inequitable system of pay that affects 6,000 employees.

Similar reasoning would seem to apply to the CBC. Since both the Corporation and its 570 secretaries stand to benefit, the Task Force recommends that the Corporation:

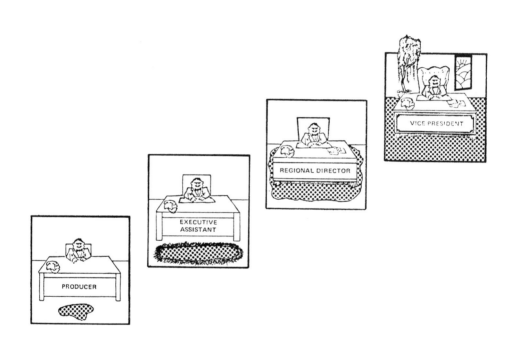

Fig. 56   Rug ranking - guess which boss has the best paid secretary?

SECRETARIAL PAY SURVEYS

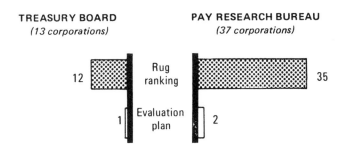

Fig. 57 *In using rug ranking, the CBC follows prevailing industry practice*

STENOGRAPHER/SECRETARY ASSIGNMENTS		
Position Title		**Level of Assignment**
Secretary to executive	F	Vice-Presidents Vice-Presidents and General Managers
Senior secretary	E-F	Assistant Vice-President Assistant General Manager Regional/Area Director Director of Radio-Canada International Director of Northern and Armed Forces Chief Engineer General Counsel
Senior secretary	E	To principals whose positions are classified within the MS VIII, IX, or higher levels, including the Executive Assistant to the President
Secretary	D or 4	To principals whose positions are classified within the MS VI or VII levels as well as Executive Assistants or Assistants to Senior Officers at the MS VIII, IX, or higher levels
Stenographer/secretary	3-4 or C-D	To principals whose positions are classified within the MS IV or V levels

Fig. 58 *A secretary's pay is determined solely by the level of the person she works for*

```
┌─────────────────────────────────────┐
│           MAIN FEATURES OF           │
│          JOB EVALUATION PLAN         │
├─────────────────────────────────────┤
│                                      │
│   — Use of six job-related factors   │
│                                      │
│        . Education                   │
│        . Experience                  │
│        . Judgment                    │
│        . Responsibility              │
│        . Relationships               │
│        . Resourcefulness             │
│                                      │
│   — Ranking of each factor by order of│
│     importance on particular job     │
│                                      │
│   — Allocation of points to each factor│
│                                      │
│   — Computation of total score for each│
│     position                         │
│                                      │
└─────────────────────────────────────┘
```

Fig. 59   Job evaluation determines the pay level of all positions in the CBC, except secretaries

```
┌─────────────────────────────────────┐
│           ROYAL COMMISSION           │
│          ON STATUS OF WOMEN          │
├─────────────────────────────────────┤
│  "We would also like to draw attention to a │
│  practice that we consider an unfair way of  │
│  establishing the pay for a traditionally female│
│  occupation.  The level that a secretary can │
│  reach is based on the level of the person she│
│  works for rather than the duties she performs.│
│  In our view, this practice of 'rug ranking' │
│  seriously infringes on the rights of individuals│
│  to equitable treatment and places secretaries│
│  in a position in which their pay is dependent│
│  on the pay received by others.  Therefore, we│
│  recommend that the positions of secretaries │
│  in the federal Public Service be classified by│
│  one of the methods used for other classes in│
│  the federal Public Service."                │
└─────────────────────────────────────┘
```

Fig. 60   The Royal Commission recommended the abolition of rug ranking 4 years ago

MAIN FEATURES OF
PLANNED PUBLIC SERVICE
SECRETARIAL RATING PLAN

— Job description for each of seven classification levels
  of secretaries

— Ranking of individuals according to skills/responsibilities
  required for particular level

    . Participation

    . Expertise

    . Skills

    . Knowledge

    . Responsibility for contacts

    . Physical effort

    . Mental effort

    . Responsibility for work of others

    . Supervisory responsibility

    . Advisory responsibility

— Assignment to boss dependent on matching individual
  skills with job requirements, rather than status of boss

— Compensation will depend on level achieved, rather than
  status of boss

— Promotion will depend on gaining new skills or being
  able to assume more responsibilities, rather than promotion of boss

*Fig. 61 The federal Public Service will finally implement a new evaluation
plan for its 6,000 secretaries in mid-1975*

20. Abolish rug ranking, and institute instead a job evaluation plan for stenographers and secretaries.

21. Use the project team approach for designing and implementing the plan, working at the same English Services location as for the advancement project.

The project team, which would study and adapt the Public Service plan, would also need to work closely with CUPE (O & P), so that implications with respect to the union agreement are fully considered. Implementation would have to be carried out with care, and in full cooperation with the team working on advancement for the same group. For example, jobs that need to be downgraded would pose a particular difficulty. The Public Service plans to allow the persons now occupying these jobs to remain in their present pay categories, advancing normally through all the salary steps; they would hire at the new rates when vacancies occur. The project team might well conclude that the CBC should follow the same practice.

The Public Service estimates suggest that about one-quarter or one-third of the secretarial positions might be found to need an average upgrading of one level, with a smaller number being downgraded. Assuming that CBC positions might follow the same pattern, and assuming an average differential of $800 between levels, we would estimate that the additional annual cost of adopting our recommendations would be approximately $150,000.

TREATMENT ON THE JOB

After investigating advancement and compensation, we looked at how secretaries are treated by their fellow workers on a day-to-day basis. It is of course impossible to examine treatment on the job by looking at facts and figures; but the secretaries' comments that we heard across the country, some of which are used to introduce this chapter, amply illustrate the depth of frustration that is felt. And, from the opposite point of view, the kinds of comments made by many CBC men showed the attitudes that have influenced the secretaries' working climate and added to the frustration.

We recognize the dangers in relying on personal examples, which are bound to be subjective. Nevertheless, we feel confident in stating two conclusions; first, the attitudinal climate in which many secretaries work is both demotivating and demoralizing; and second, a number of specific practices by supervisors, no one of which is in itself particularly significant, combine to devalue the secretary's job in the eyes of others. As a result, many secretaries feel that they are ill treated.

Looking at the first of these conclusions, the attitudes expressed by men across the country can be summarized in four statements: secretarial work is unimportant; physical appearance counts a good deal; the secretary exists to serve her boss; and secretarial work is unsuitable for men. Not surprisingly, the secretaries respond in parallel fashion: my work is not valued; my appearance, not my ability, is what counts; I am the personal servant of a man, not an employee of the Corporation; I am being discriminated against because I am a woman.

With regard to the second conclusion, it was quite clear that three specific practices, resulting from men's attitudes and the vagueness of the job responsibilities, quite naturally create resentment. First, assistance with personal business is asked and expected of many secretaries. Typical demands are picking up laundry, buying gifts for friends, getting theatre tickets, and typing personal correspondence. Second, getting or making coffee has come to be widely viewed as a job duty, rather than a favour. And finally, an undoubted lack of common courtesy too frequently prevails; an order, rather than a request, initiates a task.

In order to improve the treatment that secretaries receive in day-to-day working relationships with their bosses, the Task Force recommends that the Corporation:

22. Develop detailed job descriptions for secretaries, starting with the English Services pilot project.

Detailed job descriptions will help to clarify the expectations of both boss and secretary. If serving coffee and collecting laundry, for example, are part of the job, then these duties should be included in the job description. Since development of job descriptions will be closely linked with the establishment of an evaluation system to replace rug ranking, these two projects should go hand in hand.

23. Seek to increase the number of men engaged in secretarial functions.

The stereotype of the female secretary will be broken down only when there are more male secretaries. The Corporation should encourage the hiring of male secretaries, by including specific provisions with respect to secretaries as part of the overall policy and guidelines on job access, and by asking employment personnel to seek out men as well as women as secretarial candidates.

24. Ensure that a session on boss-secretary relationships is incorporated in supervisory training.

A key to solving the attitude problem is to ensure that supervisors are aware of the way their behaviour is perceived by their secretaries, and the negative effects of that behaviour on morale and work. The inclusion of a session on boss-secretary relationships in supervisory training will, at the very least, make insensitive supervisors aware that the Corporation is concerned about the problem, even if ingrained attitudes can only be changed over time.

In this chapter, we have described some of the weaknesses of the secretarial job as it exists in the CBC, as well as the negative and demoralizing climate in which many secretaries work. We have recommended projects to clarify their duties, to help them to advance in the areas for which they are qualified, and to measure the value of their work so that their remuneration will be based on the standards used for other employees. We have also urged that the people they work for make an effort to see the relationship more objectively, and we believe that the resulting changes will vastly improve both the usefulness to the Corporation of its secretaries, and their satisfaction with the job.

In the next chapter, we shall be less concerned with attitudes and stereotypes, as we look at the facts and figures which show how women and men in the Corporation are paid, and at the fringe benefits they receive.

* * * * *

MANAGEMENT RESPONSE

The Task Force has made seven separate recommendations relating to the secretarial position: two on advancement, two on rug ranking, and three on treatment on the job. Although these recommendations are aimed at three separate sets of problems, all but two have a common starting point - namely, a project to conduct an in-depth examination of the secretarial position, leading to an integrated series of action steps in each of the problem areas. Six of these recommendations management accepts in full, and one is accepted with a slight qualification. In doing so, we would draw employees' attention to the implementation dates - specifically late 1975 and early 1976 - suggested by the Task Force in Chapter 7 on the overall equal opportunity program.

> **18. Establish an action program that gives special encouragement to qualified secretaries to advance into administration and production.**
> Accepted in full.

> **19. Undertake, as a first step, a project in an English Services region outside Toronto to design and implement new advancement paths.**
> Accepted in part. We agree to undertake a project in an English Services region. However, we would like to consider Toronto as a possible location for the project because the widest range of secretarial functions and the majority of ESD's secretaries are there.

> **20. Abolish rug ranking, and institute instead a job evaluation plan for stenographers and secretaries.**
> Accepted in full.

> **21. Use the project team approach for designing and implementing the plan, working at the same English Services location as for the advancement project.**
> Accepted in full.

> **22. Develop detailed job descriptions for secretaries, starting with the English Services pilot project.**
> Accepted in full.

The other two recommendations are also accepted in full.

23. Seek to increase the number of men engaged in secretarial functions.
Accepted in full. While we agree completely with the recommendation, we would urge staff not to expect significant increases in the number of male secretaries in the near future, primarily because in the labour market today there appear to be very few men who both desire a secretarial position and are qualified to fill it.

24. Ensure that a session on boss-secretary relationships is incorporated in supervisory training.
Accepted in full.

5. COMPENSATION

An examination of the way in which men and women are paid is a basic component of any study of the status of the sexes. The Task Force examined three areas of compensation for CBC staff*. The first area was concerned with salaries, both at the time of entry and when working on a continuing basis. And the second dealt with the other main component of compensation - that is, benefits, including group life, hospital and medical, pensions, travel, and voluntary accident insurances. Finally, we also looked at allowances, for relocation, travel, and the like.

SALARIES

In deciding salaries, the governing principle is "equal pay for equal work", and it is certainly in the Corporation's interest to make absolutely sure that this principle is followed. For one thing, the CBC is clearly interested in maintaining equity in an area that is so important to its employees. Moreover, since 1971 the Canada Labour Code has made the payment of different wages illegal, when men and women in the same federal organization perform the same or similar work, under the same or similar working conditions, or on jobs requiring the same or similar skill, effort, and responsibility.

In the United States, violation of equal pay legislation has proved to be very expensive. Many "class actions" are pending, and there have already been some settlements, including the case in which American Telephone & Telegraph was forced to pay over $30 million in back wages to its female employees. While it is not possible to bring class actions at this time in Canada, the CBC certainly would not welcome a rash of individual suits.

Because the principle is so important, the Task Force felt it was vital to examine the issue of equality of pay extremely closely. To begin with, we recognized that several legitimate factors can cause variances in rates of pay between women and men in the CBC. These include differences in responsibilities in the same position category; for example, two people may be performing the same function at two locations, but one may be handling a large and complex department while another is supervising a quite small operation. The way different supervisors assign responsibilities will also sometimes make one job more "valuable" than another, as will the talents of the individual occupying it. Background and experience, CBC seniority and tenure on the job, and, in some jobs, performance, are also reflected in rates of pay.

---

* Our mandate extended only to staff; we therefore did not examine compensation for contract personnel (shadow establishment), except for producers on continuing contracts. Producers paid out of direct program funds are not included.

106

These factors make it impossible simply to average men's and women's salaries in various job groupings and reach conclusions. Rather, we had to examine individual positions. But in doing so we looked for those with at least five employees of each sex - a difficult task, because of the extent of job segregation in the CBC - in order to obtain statistically meaningful pay comparisons. We looked for what seemed to be significant trends - for example, major pay differences (we arbitrarily took as "major" more than 5 percent); and patterns of discrimination within job categories, departments, or locations. While we were made aware of instances of seemingly unfair treatment of individual women, we did not draw our main conclusions from scattered examples.

Starting Pay

First, we were anxious to establish whether men and women with similar background and experience are hired at equal salaries. Differences in hiring rates are important for two reasons; they are hard to correct later, given the step-by-step progression of union jobs and the Corporation's salary administration practices in the more discretionary areas such as management. What is more, a failure to hire at equal levels is contrary to the spirit of the equal opportunity policy.

In our interviews, we quickly found a widespread belief among women that the Corporation gives the men it hires "top dollar", while the women are short-changed. Women not only assume that this is so, but see the reasons as twofold: that the men who do the hiring assume that a male employee needs the money, while a woman does not; and that the male applicant, perhaps having more confidence and experience in negotiating, insists on the best deal possible. The women, on the other hand, see themselves as being so eager to get into broadcasting that they will accept and even feel grateful - at the time - for whatever is offered.

To see whether the perception was accurate, we examined the records for 1973. Of the 850 employees hired to fill permanent staff jobs in that year, the 483 men were hired at salaries averaging one-third higher than the 367 women (Figure 62). However, very few job categories in which there were hirings included both sexes (Figure 63), and only these categories could indicate whether or not there were inequalities. In these positions, we found no discrimination overall (Figure 64) - but in higher paying positions, including several non-union jobs, there was a tendency to pay women less (Figure 65). In some cases, age and presumed experience probably accounted for the difference; but there were a few positions where there was no apparent reason for the variance (Figure 66).

After examining the available evidence, then (Figure 67), the Task Force concluded that, in general, the CBC does not discriminate against women in setting salary levels at entry. However, there are tendencies to pay women less in higher paying jobs, where supervisors have greater discretion. Supervisors, who are naturally anxious to negotiate the best price, often seem to assume that women have less financial need; and they sometimes try to make women feel that they are *"lucky to get a job at the CBC"*. And

NEW HIRINGS: AVERAGE SALARIES
— 1973 —

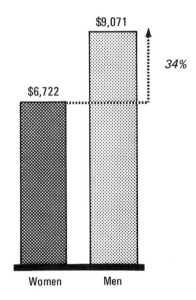

Fig. 62   For newly hired employees, men's average salary was one-third higher

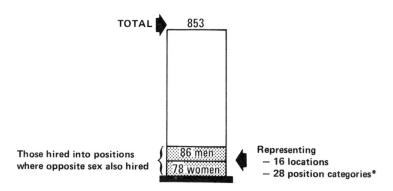

1973 HIRINGS

TOTAL ▶ 853

Those hired into positions
where opposite sex also hired

86 men
78 women

Representing
— 16 locations
— 28 position categories*

* — Assumes category is different for each location

Fig. 63   Relatively few hirings involved both sexes

COMPARISON OF 1973 ENTERING SALARIES
WHERE BOTH SEXES WERE INVOLVED

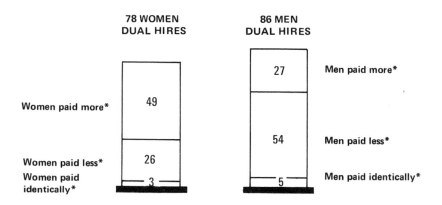

78 WOMEN
DUAL HIRES

86 MEN
DUAL HIRES

Women paid more*   49

Women paid less*   26
Women paid
identically*   3

Men paid more*   27

Men paid less*   54

Men paid identically*   5

* — On average

*Fig. 64   An overall look at hirings indicates that there was no pattern of dis-
crimination*

109

1973 ENTERING SALARIES

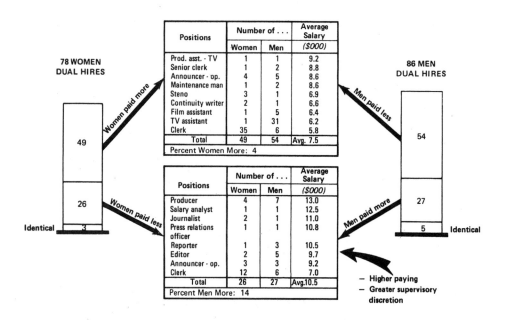

78 WOMEN DUAL HIRES

49

26

3 — Identical

Women paid more

Women paid less

Positions	Number of . . .		Average Salary
	Women	Men	($000)
Prod. asst. - TV	1	1	9.2
Senior clerk	1	2	8.8
Announcer - op.	4	5	8.6
Maintenance man	1	2	8.6
Steno	3	1	6.9
Continuity writer	2	1	6.6
Film assistant	1	5	6.4
TV assistant	1	31	6.2
Clerk	35	6	5.8
Total	**49**	**54**	**Avg. 7.5**
Percent Women More: 4			

Positions	Number of . . .		Average Salary
	Women	Men	($000)
Producer	4	7	13.0
Salary analyst	1	1	12.5
Journalist	2	1	11.0
Press relations officer	1	1	10.8
Reporter	1	3	10.5
Editor	2	5	9.7
Announcer - op.	3	3	9.2
Clerk	12	6	7.0
Total	**26**	**27**	**Avg.10.5**
Percent Men More: 14			

86 MEN DUAL HIRES

Men paid less

54

27

5 — Identical

Men paid more

— Higher paying
— Greater supervisory discretion

Fig. 65   Men were paid more, on average, in all hirings above $10,000

110

POSITIONS INTO WHICH BOTH SEXES WERE HIRED
AT OR ABOVE $10,000
—1973—

LOCATION	POSITION	MEN			WOMEN			PERCENT-AGE HIGHER SALARY (MEN'S)
		Number Hired	Average Salary	Average Age	Number Hired	Average Salary	Average Age	
Toronto Region	1. Reporter	3	11.5	35	1	9.3	25	23
Toronto ESD	2. Press Relations Officer	1	11.2	25	1	10.3	26	9
	3. Producer	4	15.6	30	2	14.5	34	8
Montreal FSD	4. Salary Analyst	1	13.0	32	1	12.0	33	8
Moncton	5. Announcer-Operator	2	10.0	27	2	9.2	25	9
Ottawa Area	6. Editor	5	10.1	26	2	9.4	24	9
Winnipeg	7. Producer	3	11.6	46	2	10.4	28	12
TOTAL		19			11			
AVERAGE			11.9	32		10.9	28	10.2

◀ *Not explained by age difference,
presumed to mean greater experience*

Fig. 66   There is no apparent reason for the discrepancies in a number of higher paying jobs

111

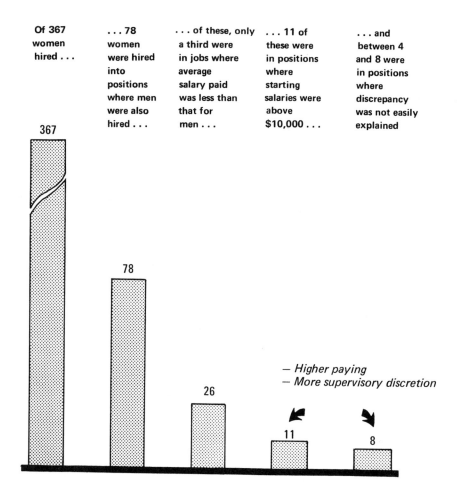

Of 367 women hired . . .

. . . 78 women were hired into positions where men were also hired . . .

. . . of these, only a third were in jobs where average salary paid was less than that for men . . .

. . . 11 of these were in positions where starting salaries were above $10,000 . . .

. . . and between 4 and 8 were in positions where discrepancy was not easily explained

367

78

26

11

8

— Higher paying
— More supervisory discretion

Fig. 67   There was no discrimination in entry level salaries, but there was a tendency to pay women less in higher paying jobs

some women do lack the confidence needed to conduct tough salary negotiations with a prospective employer. The result of these tendencies is occasional starting salary differences that run counter to the spirit of equal opportunity; what is more, they "lock in" discriminatory pay levels thereafter.

Equal Pay for Equal Work?

Many women doubt that, in the instances where both sexes occupy similar posts, the Corporation consistently applies the same standards to women's and men's pay after entry. Most believe that men's and women's pay is close to parity in the majority of jobs, but some suspect that this is largely because most jobs are unionized (Figure 68). Where there is more flexibility - as in management and to some degree among producers - women believe that there may be discrimination.

However, though they agree for the most part that pay is equal, they frequently add that the problem is unequal work, in the same position. They point to supervisors who set more exacting standards for female employees - being stricter with women about arrival and departure times, for example. One of the most common complaints concerns the unwritten requirement for women to retain some or all of their secretarial duties when they are promoted to a job that, when done by a man, does not involve typing. Another contention that arose several times was that positions are downgraded when a woman succeeds a man, with a lower salary grouping being justified by some slight reallocation of duties.

Where *equal pay* was concerned, to check these impressions as far as possible against the facts, we reviewed current salaries for every position category in which both sexes are represented (Figure 69). Overall, men are more highly paid in roughly two-thirds of the categories. On the other hand, more than two-thirds of these jobs have so few of the minority sex that the statistics are not reliable. Of the remaining one-third, only half involve major differences in pay (Figure 70). Where such differences do occur, seniority figures, which indicate whether age and experience account for the inequality, show only three categories (designer, announcer-producer, and information services assistant) in which men receive significantly higher pay for no apparent reason (Figure 71).

The two categories most frequently mentioned in interviews and briefs were management jobs and producers' positions. With regard to producers, there appear at first to be some inequalities. The average salaries and seniority of women producers in French Services in Montreal seem to show that they are underpaid, relative to their seniority (Figure 72). However, seniority shows only how long they have been in the CBC; we found that the women's tenure in the jobs in question is actually much shorter than that of the men. In fact, on average they are more than fairly treated. Additionally, the higher average pay received by men is justified by the greater responsibilities they carry (Figure 73).

Turning to management jobs, a similar comparison was made of salaries in MS II. This level was chosen because, initially, figures suggest a discrep-

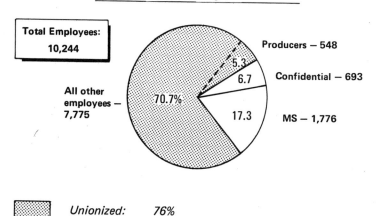

AFFILIATION OF CBC EMPLOYEES
— At June 30, 1974 —
(percentage)

Total Employees: 10,244

Producers — 548

Confidential — 693

All other employees — 7,775

70.7%

5.3

6.7

17.3

MS — 1,776

Unionized: 76%

Nonunionized: 24%

Fig. 68   Widespread pay discrimination would be surprising, given the extent of unionization

EXAMPLE

POSITION	MEN				WOMEN			
	Number	Average Salary	Average Age	Average Seniority	Number	Average Salary	Average Age	Average Seniority
Translator	7	$17,732	54	14	2	$16,617	41	9
Sales Service Representative	15	13,043	39	15	7	12,771	35	4
Assistant Costume Designer	9	11,446	41	7	15	11,586	37	6
Senior Clerk	107	11,407	38	13	101	10,999	40	11

Fig. 69   The Task Force reviewed current salaries for every position category in which both sexes are represented

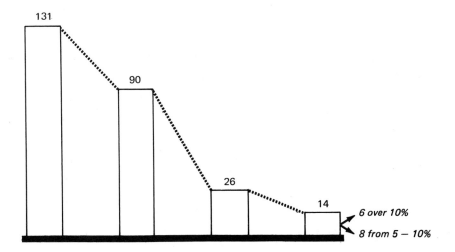

131 position
categories involve
both sexes . . .

. . . of these, men
are paid more
in 90 . . .

. . . but only 26 of
these have significant
numbers of each
sex . . .

. . . and among
them, only 14
involve major
difference in pay

131

90

26

14

6 over 10%

8 from 5 – 10%

*Fig. 70 Of 131 position categories that include both sexes, men are paid
significantly more in 14*

CATEGORIES WHERE MEN ARE
SIGNIFICANTLY HIGHER PAID

POSITION	PERCENTAGE HIGHER SALARY	PERCENTAGE SENIORITY DIFFERENCE	
Registry Clerk	5.4	250.0	
Designer	5.7	0.0	◄
Press Relations Officer	6.8	350.0	
Reporter	7.0	67.0	
Radio Production Assistant	8.6	57.0	
Associate Designer	8.7	33.0	
Announcer-Producer (RCI)	9.0	(16.0)	◄
Journalist	9.6	66.0	
Administrative Assistant	10.3	100.0	
Producer	11.3	20.0	
Editor	14.5	500.0	
Announcer-Operator	15.0	300.0	
Announcer	18.5	367.0	
Information Services Assistant	19.5	(25.0)	◄

From 5% to 10% Higher

Over 10% Higher

◄ Not explained by seniority

Fig. 71   Seniority explains all but three of the "suspicious" cases

116

HIGHER PAY AND SENIORITY — MEN
(Percentage)

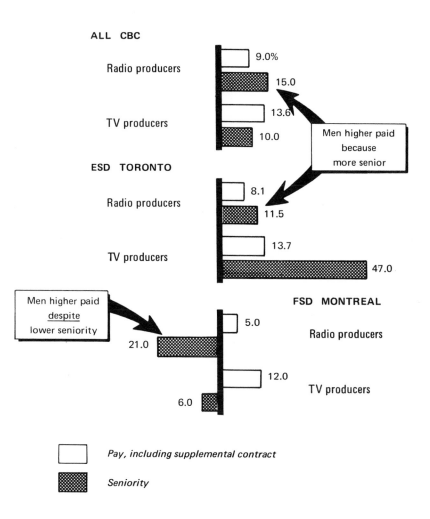

ALL CBC

Radio producers — 9.0% / 15.0

TV producers — 13.6 / 10.0

Men higher paid because more senior

ESD TORONTO

Radio producers — 8.1 / 11.5

TV producers — 13.7 / 47.0

FSD MONTREAL

Men higher paid despite lower seniority

Radio producers — 5.0 / 21.0

TV producers — 12.0 / 6.0

☐ Pay, including supplemental contract

▨ Seniority

Fig. 72 Initial comparisons of pay and seniority indicated a problem in FSD Montreal

Despite lower seniority, higher pay is explainable by higher tenure on the job . . .

. . . and by types of shows produced, which suggest men carry greater responsibility

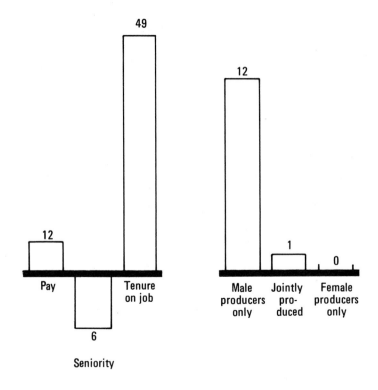

FSD TV PRODUCERS*
(percentage higher pay, seniority, and tenure — men)

49

12

6

Pay

Tenure on job

Seniority

**FSD TV SPECIALS
1974 – 1975****

12

1

0

Male producers only

Jointly pro- duced

Female producers only

* — *Similar figures for FSD radio producers*

** — *Six or fewer episodes per year; where producer assignments are now known, specials in Emissions Feminines not yet assigned; excluding music*

Fig. 73   In FSD TV, the pay difference seems to be justified

ancy there (Figure 74) but, once again, a closer look tells a different story. In MS positions, not all employees advance at the same rate. Improvements in salary are dependent on merit increases, which are at the discretion of the supervisor. Thus, two employees starting at the bottom of the scale may climb the salary scale at a different rate. And, of course, not all employees do start at the bottom of the scale; many of them are promoted from unionized jobs, and by agreement must be paid a certain percentage more than they made in the previous job, including overtime. Since many more men than women move from unionized jobs with regular overtime, more of them will start higher up the MS II scale. This may help to explain why, although only 59 percent of men have been in MS II for as much as 3 years, 77 percent of them are at or above salary standard, while, in the case of the women, 44 percent have at least 3 years' tenure, but only 33 percent of them have reached salary standard (Figure 75). However, while by no means providing cast-iron evidence of discrimination, the facts do indicate that even within a single management-specialist grouping, women generally are paid less than men with comparable tenure.

On the *pay* side of "equal pay for equal work", then, the Task Force concluded that the CBC generally does pay women and men equally when the two hold the same or approximately the same position. But there are tendencies to pay women less, particularly in positions in which there is some flexibility in the administration of salaries. Men are paid more than women in 68 percent of position categories in which both sexes are represented, and some anomalies in pay are not explained by differences in seniority (e.g., announcer-producers in Radio-Canada International). Finally, in some groups in the MS scale, significant differences within the same range are not explained by tenure on the job.

The *equal work* side of the pay equation is much harder to pin down. The statistics do not contain any clues; and different people see any situation in different ways. But a great number of CBC women are firmly convinced that they are forced to do extra tasks not required of their male colleagues, that their jobs are classified at lower levels than those of men, or that the standards of performance are stricter and more demanding. Figure 76 shows some typical comments.

Such observations, repeated again and again, lead to the conclusion that there are a significant number of situations in which more is required of women than of men, for the same pay. The Task Force was given at least 50 specific examples of greater demands being made of women than of their male colleagues. While it was impossible to investigate these claims individually, both the consistent nature of the complaints and the confirming evidence in interviews with men led us to believe that there is a real tendency to supervise women more strictly, and to add small duties not included in their job descriptions.

Recommendations

In the area of salaries, then, the Task Force found that although CBC women have a very negative view of CBC's practices, actual salary discrimination

MS EMPLOYEES BELOW SALARY STANDARD:
GROUPS I – III*
(percentage)

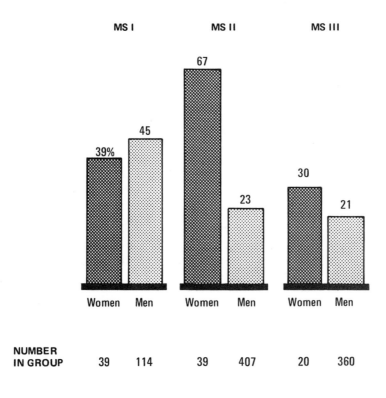

| NUMBER IN GROUP | 39 | 114 | 39 | 407 | 20 | 360 |

* — *Represents 86% of all women MS*

Fig. 74 Initial comparisons of compensation with salary standard indicated a problem in MS II

MEN   WOMEN

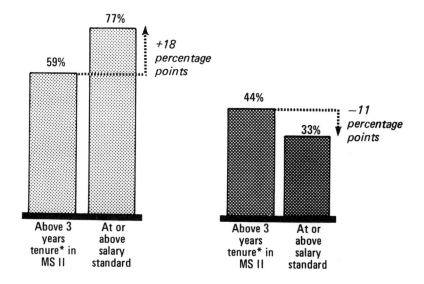

* — Normal progression is about 3 years from minimum to standard

Fig. 75 The possible pay problem in MS II is only partly explained by tenure on the job

Many feel that they carry duties beyond a man's . . .

. . . or that their jobs are wrongly classified compared to a male's . . .

. . . or that standards of per-formance are more demanding

"In order to take a big step forward, I was obliged to retain all my former secretarial duties"

"I'm considered a cutter, but my assistant and I do the work of 18 designers"

"I'm disciplined if I'm the slightest bit late for work, while the men in our section seem to be able to come and go as they please"

"Mine was a lateral transfer to the position of _____, replacing a male, Group 6 . . . 9 years later, I am still Group 5"

"Women have to be twice as good to succeed in this department"

Fig. 76   Many women clearly believe that work is not equal

is rare. Our recommendations are aimed at eliminating the occasional cases of discrimination that do occur, maintaining the generally favourable record on starting salaries and on equality of pay thereafter, and in so doing reducing the negative impression of the Corporation's compensation practices among its female employees.

The Task Force therefore recommends that the Corporation:

25. Develop and distribute to all employees an overall equal pay policy and guidelines for its administration.

The equal pay policy document should make the CBC position completely clear, and the guidelines should spell out exactly how the policy is to be interpreted. Figure 77 shows the kind of memorandum we envisage.

The Task Force also recommends that the Corporation:

26. Request, following the issuance of that policy, that all supervisors review the salaries of men and women in identical position categories, to determine whether differences are justified.

27. Review annually all entry salaries and position-by-position comparisons, and follow up apparent anomalies with the supervisors concerned.

Once the policy document is issued, the Director of Compensation at Head Office should instruct all supervisors to carry out an immediate comparative review of men's and women's salaries. Subsequently, this review should be undertaken annually; the follow-up on each occasion will focus attention on the policy, and help to bring an end to all discrimination in pay.

28. Incorporate materials on unconscious discrimination in salary administration into general supervisory training.

We would expect our first three compensation recommendations to have an immediate effect; however, on a long-term basis, the best means of attack on discrimination in salary administration is to tackle it at source through supervisory training. Many of the instances of unequal treatment that do exist are not the result of conscious discrimination; for example, the supervisor may be in the habit of assuming that a woman needs less money than a man, and as a matter of course may come up with a lower figure. The way to avoid such behaviour is to make the supervisor aware not only that he is the captive of a stereotype, but that to act on such assumptions is both wrong and illegal.

One final word on salaries: The Task Force noted that the most deeply felt complaints of pay discrimination came from women on contract. While their status was not within our mandate, we received several briefs from free-

EXAMPLE

CBC POLICY MEMORANDUM: EQUAL PAY

The Canada Labour Code prohibits differences in wages between male and female employees . . . Clearly, then, CBC policy is to pay women and men equally for work of equivalent value.

The purpose of this memorandum is to assist supervisors in administering this policy. To this end, the document deals with:

Hiring

1. How to balance CBC equal pay policy against the understandable desire to negotiate the lowest possible salary

Thereafter

1. Factors that are to be considered in determining pay, including:

— Qualifications

— Performance

— Etc.

2. Factors that are not to be considered, including:

— Assumed need for income

— Marital status

— Etc.

Fig. 77   An equal pay policy should make the CBC's position clear, and provide guidance to supervisors

lance women, and a number were included on interview schedules - usually because they were the only women much involved in programs in certain locations. Discrimination in pay was the problem they raised most frequently, and with great intensity. We therefore have a fifth recommendation regarding compensation:

29. Conduct a separate examination of the pay of contract personnel.

We propose that the Director of Compensation and the Director of the Office of Equal Opportunity should jointly examine the pay practices governing contract personnel. Such an examination would involve at least five steps:

1. Collect data on pay practices and fees actually paid to men and women for doing the same or similar work

2. Identify apparent anomalies

3. Follow up to determine the underlying facts

4. Estimate the extent of discrimination

5. Recommend corrective action, if required.

BENEFITS

The Corporation's two most important benefit plans - Group Life Insurance and the Pension Plan - are mandatory for all staff. It is more than 4 years since the Royal Commission on the Status of Women invited Crown Corporations to remove the inequalities in these plans (Recommendation 49, Report of the Royal Commission). In the CBC, while there has been some discussion with the Staff Consultative Committee, no action has yet been taken to eliminate the sex-based differences that are part of the two plans.

Group Life Insurance

All CBC employees must buy Group Life Insurance, with the amount specified as a condition of employment. If the employee is male, the amount of coverage depends on both sex and marital status. If the employee is female, the amount is determined by sex alone - unless the woman happens to be a single parent. A female employee must buy insurance coverage that is roughly equal to her yearly salary. A single man must buy coverage equal to twice his salary; and a married man must buy coverage equal to three times his salary. A single parent, male or female, may opt to have the same coverage as a married man. As someone put it, "If you're a woman, you can only be classified as married if you're single!" Figure 78 sets out these somewhat confusing facts in tabular form. Despite the differences in amounts of coverage that various employee groups either may or must buy, a uniform rate - $0.47 per month per $1,000 coverage - applies to everyone*.

* For the CBC's contribution to the costs of the plan, the differences are based not on sex, but on marital status. The Corporation pays a flat rate of $2.26 per month for each single employee, and $4.52 for each married person.

	CBC GROUP LIFE PLAN		
	Women	Single Men	Married Men and Single Parents**
COVERAGE SCHEDULE*	1 x salary	2 x salary	3 x salary

EXAMPLES OF COVERAGE			
$5,000 – $5,999 salary	$6,000	$12,000	$23,000
$10,000 – $10,999 salary	$11,000	$22,000	$37,000
$15,000 – $15,999 salary	$16,000	$32,000	$48,000

* — *Approximate, as coverage is weighted to provide greater protection for married men and single parents earning less than $13,000*

** — *3 x coverage is voluntary for single parents, required for married men*

Fig. 78 *A woman can only obtain as much group life insurance as a man if she is a single parent*

Some examples will help to illustrate how the sex-based differences in the Group Life Plan affect people in different family situations. Consider the case of the male employee whose wife also earns a living. They are childless, and the wife is not financially dependent on her husband. He is nonetheless obliged to insure himself for three times his salary, because it is assumed from his marital status that he has dependents. In contrast, a woman in this situation would be obliged to take only one times coverage.

Or take the married female employee with two or three children, whose husband works in a small business that does not provide group insurance. She can purchase only the equivalent of a year's salary in insurance, though she might well want to provide more protection for her family at group rates. If she and her husband could trade employers, they would be much better off.

Then there is the bachelor with no dependents, who must purchase the equivalent of double his yearly salary in insurance, whereas a single woman in the same circumstances is forced to take only half that amount. Turning the tables around, there is the single woman with dependent parents who is restricted to coverage of one times salary, while a man in the identical situation has two times the protection.

It is not surprising, then, that nearly all CBC employees we spoke with objected to differences based on sex in the Group Life Insurance Plan. And as a matter of principle, the Task Force believes that these differences should be eliminated. We therefore recommend that the Corporation:

30. Equalize coverage under the Group Life Plan, within 9 months.

Set coverage at 2 x salary for single employees, male and female; for married employees and single parents, male and female, 3 x salary

Make the new levels of coverage a condition of employment for new staff members

Allow present female employees to opt for the new plan or remain with the present coverage.

Equalization, under the present system of sharing the costs, would cost the Corporation little, either in percentage or in actual dollars (Figure 79). The burden would fall mainly on married women employees, whose average costs would increase fivefold, with only a tripling of coverage (Figure 80).

Joining the equalized plan should become a condition of employment for future employees; those now on staff should be given an option - partly because some women might resent having a change forced on them, and partly because it is doubtful whether the CBC could retroactively change a condition of employment without a vote of the staff affected.

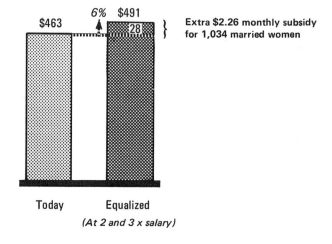

ANNUAL GROUP LIFE COSTS
(thousands of dollars)

$463   *6%* $491

28

Extra $2.26 monthly subsidy
for 1,034 married women

Today   Equalized
(At 2 and 3 x salary)

Fig. 79   Equalization would cost the CBC little

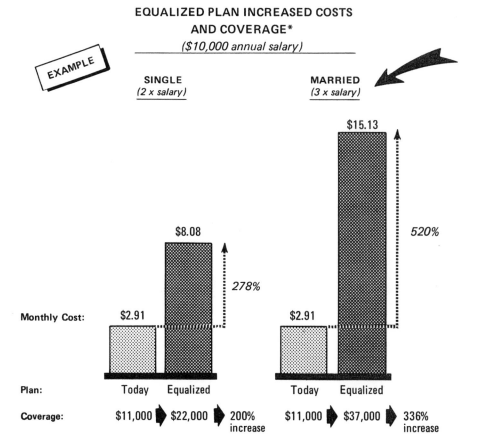

EQUALIZED PLAN INCREASED COSTS
AND COVERAGE*
($10,000 annual salary)

EXAMPLE

SINGLE
(2 x salary)

MARRIED
(3 x salary)

$15.13

$8.08

520%

278%

Monthly Cost: $2.91 $2.91

Plan: Today   Equalized   Today   Equalized

Coverage: $11,000 ▶ $22,000 ▶ 200% $11,000 ▶ $37,000 ▶ 336%
                              increase   increase

* — *For current employees who elect equalized plan*

Fig. 80   The cost to married women would increase fivefold, with only a tripling of coverage

Figure 81 shows a schedule that would allow the new plan to be introduced within 9 months. It is important that such a deadline be set, because while changes in the plan have been under discussion for years, no action has been taken. With the overwhelming support that this proposal for equalization received from staff across the country, a quick response will be welcomed; removal of differences based on sex would be tangible evidence of the Corporation's commitment to equal opportunity.

In addition to problems created by the sex-based differences in Group Life coverage, many employees, both male and female, find that the current plan forces them to take coverage that they do not need, and others feel that they are not able to obtain extra coverage that they may require. An example of the former, mentioned earlier, is the single man without dependents who is forced to take two times coverage. A large majority of employees would like more flexibility, by way of options, though almost all understand that a basic minimum must be mandatory in any low-cost group plan. They received with approval the suggestion of a formula such as this:

— Compulsory for all employees: 1 x salary

— Optional: 2 or 3 x salary

— Either with costs shared as at present - though on the basis of "with or without dependents" rather than "married or single" - or with full costs of the compulsory unit paid by CBC, and full optional coverage paid by the employee.

Because the investigation of options was less directly within our mandate but does represent the expressed wish of the majority of staff, we recommend that the Corporation:

31. Investigate the possibility of a later revision of the plan to introduce optional coverage.

On the basis of our talks with CBC compensation officers, it seems clear that a further change, after equalization under our first recommendation, should not cause undue administrative problems. Naturally, there are several questions that would require careful investigation: What impact would such a change have on the overall benefits package? Would rates rise if single men are permitted to elect lower coverage; if so, how much? Who would pay for what? And how would the options be administered? These questions, we suggest, should be the subject of a study to be undertaken immediately by the Director of Compensation, working with the Staff Consultative Committee.

Pension Plan

The CBC Pension Plan is also different for male and female employees (Figure 82). Women pay 1 percent of salary less than men into the plan;

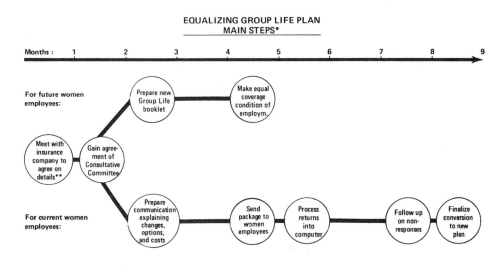

EQUALIZING GROUP LIFE PLAN
MAIN STEPS*

Months :   1   2   3   4   5   6   7   8   9

For future women
employees:

Prepare new Group Life booklet

Make equal coverage condition of employm.

Meet with insurance company to agree on details**

Gain agreement of Consultative Committee

For current women
employees:

Prepare communication explaining changes, options, and costs

Send package to women employees

Process returns into computer

Follow up on non-responses

Finalize conversion to new plan

*   −   *Responsibility of Director, Compensation*
** −   *Wording of master contract − e.g., no refinancing required because plan is experience-rated*

Fig. 81   *The group life plan could be equalized within 9 months*

131

CBC PENSION PLAN		
Payout	**Men**	**Women**
Employee pension	2% x number of years x average salary (best 5 continuous of last 10 years)	
Survivor benefits	Payments of — 50% to widow — 10% for each dependent child (up to maximum of 40%) — 20% for each orphan (up to maximum of 80%)	Pension dies with pensioner

Fig. 82   In the CBC's pension plan, women do not receive the same survivor benefits as men

they receive the same pensions as men in the same salary and seniority bracket when they retire, but do not have the same survivor benefits: the extra 1 percent that a male employee pays provides protection for his widow and any dependent children. The female employee's family gets no protection, unless she is a single parent, or her widower or dependent children can prove "need" through a means test.

Outside the Corporation, the trend is to implement the Royal Commission's recommendation regarding the elimination of sex-based differences in company superannuation plans. The Public Service is about to take action; a revision of the Superannuation Plan, removing inequalities in survivor benefits, died on the Order Paper with the dissolution of Parliament prior to the last election; however, the bill has been reintroduced during the current session. The Canada Pension Plan, which (along with the Quebec Pension Plan) now forms part of CBC coverage, is also expected to be changed in like manner during the present sitting. And several large companies, such as the Royal Bank of Canada and Bell Canada, have already made similar revisions.

The plans as they existed in the past reflected the widely practiced ban on hiring married women on full-time staff; the federal Public Service finally opened their doors to married women in 1955, and it was not until 1961 that the CBC followed suit. Thus, in the early years of the Corporation's history, provisions for "staff" were made on the assumption that employees would all be men - most of whom would probably be the heads of families - or single women. As society and the work force has changed, many organizations have been slow to alter benefit plans to suit the new situation. Reform is long overdue. Therefore the Task Force recommends that the Corporation:

32. Equalize survivor benefits:

— *Either* **join the Public Service Superannuation Plan, as has already been discussed by the CBC and Government** (enabling legislation would be necessary before a formal request could be made)

— *Or* **equalize the CBC Plan within 9 months of a negative decision on admission to the Public Service Plan.**

In either case:

— **Make the new plan a condition of employment for all future staff**

— **Give women now on staff the option of continuing with the present arrangement.**

133

If the CBC is admitted to the Public Service Plan, survivor benefits would be equalized automatically. The CBC has made inquiries about the possibility of admission, as it is aware that the plan would have a number of advantages.

For one thing, pensions would be indexed to the cost of living (there is now a ceiling of 2 percent annually on cost-of-living increases for CBC pensioners).

In addition, the "85 formula*", by which an employee whose age and years of service add up to 85 may retire without having his or her earned pension actuarily reduced, would come into play. And finally, the absorption of our scheme into that of the Public Service would remove a corporate headache, as CBC would no longer be involved in the administration of the plan.

However, it is not yet known whether the CBC will be eligible for admission; if it is, the Corporation will then have to make a formal application, which, if accepted, would mean the disappearance of the present plan and the turning over of existing funds to the Federal Government. On the other hand, the CBC may not be admitted. In that case, we believe that, immediately following a negative decision, it should set about equalizing the present plan. This, we estimate, would take about 9 months (Figure 83).

A number of employees did suggest that there be a differential in payment between employees with and without dependents. Such a difference would appear to be acceptable, provided (a) it applies equally to men and women, married and single, and (b) it does not seriously increase costs.

As with Group Life Insurance, increased costs would be borne primarily by staff women; those who elect the equalized plan will have to pay an extra 1 percent of salary. The Corporation's costs, according to a preliminary opinion by a CBC benefits consultant, would not change - though, naturally, any generosity on the Corporation's part would be most acceptable, provided it applies equally to men and women! The reasons for the "no change" opinion were that, first, the extra income to the fund would come primarily from greater payments by women employees. And second, depletion of the fund, through more payments to survivors, would probably not increase significantly; fewer than half of CBC women are married, and a large proportion of those are likely to outlive their husbands (Figure 84).

---

* We found, however, that many employees misunderstood the application of this formula; with its use, an employee must still have 35 years' service to receive maximum pension, as the formula "2 percent of average of best 5 continuous of last 10 years' salary times years of service" would still apply.

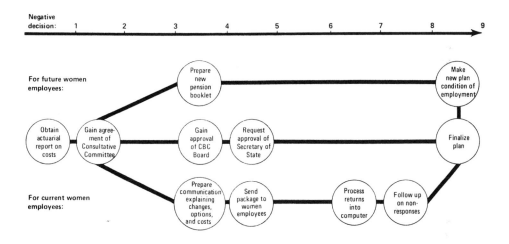

Fig. 83 If the Treasury Board decision is negative, the CBC should equalize its pension plan within 9 months

ANNUAL CONTRIBUTION
(dollars)

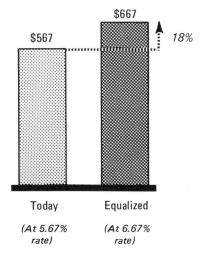

Fig. 84 *As with group life, costs of equalization would be borne primarily by women*

In our investigation, we found that many employees want the definition of *dependent* to be broadened. At present, the CBC Pension Plan limits it to *wife* and *dependent children.* But a surprising number of employees - especially single women - have other relatives (parents, brothers, sisters) whom they support. They, and many of their colleagues, believe the definition should be broadened to provide much needed survivor benefits to these individuals, as well as to be consistent with the Income Tax Act. The Task Force therefore recommends that the Corporation:

33. **Investigate the possibility of broadening the definition of dependents to that used in the Income Tax Act, with the understanding that only one adult could be named as a dependent, along with dependent children as presently defined.**

With this proviso, it is unlikely that the broadening of the definition should make any appreciable difference in costs, especially since the life expectancy of the new *dependents,* many of whom are invalids, is probably less on average than the present *widows;* and numbers of people with no dependents would be contributing to the plan.

The term *spouse* - which would replace *wife* or *widow* - should, again in accordance with the definitions in the Income Tax Act, include established common-law relationships. In its investigation of the impact of the broadening of this term, plus allowing for naming a dependent adult *other* than the spouse, the CBC should study carefully: whether rates would change, and by how much; who would pay for what; and how the new definition would be administered.

All changes in both Group Life Insurance and Pension Plans would be worked out between the office of the Director, Compensation, and the Staff Consultative Committee.

ALLOWANCES

Although current practice appears to be fairly equitable, the wording of the regulations regarding Northern Allowances, and Transfer and Removal Allowances, is at present discriminatory. The sex-based difference in the Northern Allowance occurs in the definition (currently being revised by Corporate Personnel) of *dependents;* the allowances vary in amount according to the number of dependents, and one category of dependents is defined as *wife* rather than *spouse.* The CBC woman must therefore prove need in order to receive the allowance for her husband; but the CBC man receives the wife's allowance, regardless of whether or not she is gainfully employed.

The difference in the Transfer and Removal Allowance is also contained in the definition of whose expenses are to be reimbursed. According to certain parts of the policy, reimbursement is to be provided for the employee and *wife* rather than for the employee and *spouse.* If this policy were followed to the letter, CBC women employees would be denied reimbursement for their husbands although, in practice, the policy is said usually to be administered without regard to sex.

The Task Force recommends that the Corporation:

34. **Implement immediately the Corporate Personnel revision of the definition of dependents in the Northern
Allowance policy.**

35. **Change all references from** *wife* **to** *spouse* **in both
policy and forms that describe Transfer and Removal
Allowances.**

To summarize: In the area of compensation, we found that the CBC generally treats men and women equally in matters of salary for the same job.
The two most important staff benefit plans differentiate between employees
on the basis of sex, and certain allowance regulations are potentially discriminatory.

Our recommendations are, therefore, aimed at maintaining the generally
good record of the CBC in salary matters, while eliminating occasional
discriminatory practices, and at removing all differences based on sex from
benefit plans and allowances.

In the next chapter, we will be considering the responsibilities of parenthood, and how they affect the employees concerned and the functioning of
the Corporation.

* * * * *

MANAGEMENT RESPONSE

The Task Force has made 11 recommendations on various aspects of compensation. All are accepted in full.

Salaries

25. **Develop and distribute to all employees an overall
equal pay policy and guidelines for its administration.**
Accepted in full.

26. **Request, following the issuance of that policy, that all
supervisors review the salaries of men and women in
identical position categories to determine whether differences are justified.**
Accepted in full.

27. **Review annually all entry salaries and position-by-
position comparisons, and follow up apparent anomalies
with the supervisors concerned.**
Accepted in full.

28. **Incorporate materials on unconscious discrimination in salary administration into general supervisory training.**
Accepted in full.

29. **Conduct a separate examination of the pay of contract personnel.**
Accepted in full. We would point out, however, that implementation of this recommendation has a lower priority to the Corporation than those pertaining to staff employees. Thus, the examination will probably not be undertaken in the immediate future, because our compensation personnel will be fully occupied with the more pressing items such as equalizing the group life plan.

Group Life

30. **Equalize coverage under the Group Life Plan within 9 months.**
Accepted in full.

31. **Investigate the possibility of a later revision of the plan to introduce optional coverage.**
Accepted in full.

Pension

32. **Equalize survivor benefits.**
Accepted in full.

33. **Investigate the possibility of broadening the definition of dependents to that used in the Income Tax Act, with the understanding that only one adult could be named as a dependent, along with dependent children as presently defined.**
Accepted in full.

Allowances

34. **Implement immediately the Corporate Personnel revision of the definition of "dependents" in the Northern Allowance policy.**
Accepted in full.

35. **Change all references from "wife" to "spouse" in both policy and forms that describe Transfer and Removal Allowances.**
Accepted in full.

6. RESPONSIBILITIES OF PARENTHOOD

Almost 40 percent of CBC women are married, and many of them have children. Some single CBC women also have children. For these employees, the demands of parenthood may conflict with the demands of the job. The concern of the Task Force was to assess the extent of this conflict; to examine its impact on equality of opportunity for women employees, and on the functioning of the Corporation; and to determine whether and how the CBC might help to resolve it.

We looked at two aspects of parenthood that pose specific problems: child-birth and child care. We quickly found that problems associated with parent-hood affect male as well as female employees, although to a lesser degree, and framed our recommendations with this fact in mind.

At the outset, it must be said that these areas were among the most con-troversial we dealt with. Fundamental issues are at stake. Attitudes and reactions depend on the individual's basic beliefs about the role of women in society, and about the respective responsibilities of governments, em-ployers, families, and individuals. As a result, these subjects were fuel for some intense arguments at open hearings and in discussion groups. Opinion does not necessarily divide along sex lines only; there is also division de-pending on the age and marital status of the employees, and on their political and religious backgrounds.

While a number of individuals take a pragmatic position *("If it will improve their morale and their work, let's see what action the CBC could take"),* opinion in most cases is highly polarized. The more traditional view is re-flected in such comments as *"Children are the sole responsibility of the parents . . ."; "The Corporation doesn't decide that an employee should get pregnant; it's not up to the employer to take responsibility after the fact . . ."; "Women should choose between being mothers and having a career . . ."; "Why should the CBC support one group of employees? What about people with aging parents? . . ."; "I raised my own kids; why shouldn't they do the same?"*

Such views were expressed by almost half of the people we met in most locations, apart from French Services Division, Montreal, where there was near unanimity in favour of CBC action. Many of the people expressing the traditional view also see any assistance from the employer as "special treatment" for women, rather than equality of opportunity.

At the other end of the spectrum, a large group of employees take the op-posite view. Most of the women's associations - like women's groups outside the CBC - place great importance on action concerning parenthood, and either child care or paid maternity and paternity leave usually appears near the top of the list of demands. Indeed, most women's groups in Canada today consider action in these matters as *the* barometer of commitment on the part of the employer to the equality of women in the work force. They point to the conclusion of the International Labour Organization of the United Nations, to the effect that assistance with problems arising from parenthood should not be considered as "special treatment", but rather as a means of equalizing women's opportunity to earn a living and build a career, on the grounds that women are at a disadvantage in the world of work because they happen to be the childbearing sex, and usually assume most of the responsibility for caring for small children. They further argue that society at large assists with the education and custodial care of children once they reach school age; that employers have traditionally given financial assistance to married men by providing protection for their dependent children; and that men may undertake parenthood without postponing advancement in their careers.

Since views amongst employees are so highly polarized, and were often expressed to us in extremely emotional terms, the Task Force tried to be especially dispassionate in examining the specific problems facing parents working for the CBC, and in estimating the impact of these "human" problems on the functioning of the Corporation.

In this spirit, we considered childbirth policies (paternity leave and maternity leave) and child care.

PATERNITY LEAVE

Before getting into the two areas of hottest debate, we should perhaps first deal with an issue within the same subject that is much more easily resolved: paternity leave. The Task Force found that many women, as well as men, see a need for paternity leave with pay. They point out that a man's family responsibilities multiply during the week of confinement (the precise timing of which can rarely be determined in advance), particularly if there are other children. Nowadays, more and more fathers are encouraged to be present at and participate in the birth; and many younger men and women place a great deal of importance on this experience. Then there are arrangements to be made for caring for other children while the mother is in hospital, as well as for short- or long-term help on her return; visits to the hospital; notification of friends and relatives; and often looking after the other children. Men find it difficult, if not impossible, to do all this and put in full days at work. In fact, most supervisors, understanding the problems, grant the new father leave with pay to look after this "domestic contingency", as allowed by the CBC's Special Leave regulations.

But the Task Force found the practice to be inconsistent, primarily because approval of leave is at the discretion of the supervisor and the personnel officer. As a result, some men receive a full week's paid leave; others - probably the majority - get 2 or 3 days; and a few are given only the time needed to take their wives to the hospital, or no leave at all.

Recognizing the reality of the need, and the injustice of such inconsistency, the Task Force recommends that the Corporation:

141

36. Establish, for employees with 1 year of service or more, a separate paid paternity leave, to be included in an overall birth policy.

37. Set the leave entitlement at 3 days.

The main advantage to separating paternity leave from Special Leave is that it allows the CBC to establish a separate childbirth policy, thereby basing its treatment of men and women on the same principles. This measure avoids compromising the flexibility of Special Leave, while still achieving consistency (Figure 85). A 3-day entitlement would cost the CBC little or nothing; 3 days appears to be the average Special Leave now granted.

MATERNITY LEAVE

Before 1970, most Canadian women who took maternity leave were without any income while they were absent. Only a handful of companies offered paid leave for the purpose of childbirth, and it was usually for from 1 to 6 weeks. Many women were also forced to resign at some time during the pregnancy; they had no way of protecting their careers, except in those rare cases covered by union agreements. In 1970, the Royal Commission on the Status of Women recommended the amendment of the Unemployment Insurance Act to provide benefits for 18 weeks, and the amendment of the Fair Employment Practices Act to prohibit the dismissal of an employee, on any grounds, during maternity leave. In 1971, the Government changed the Unemployment Insurance Act to include provision for 15 weeks of maternity benefits, and the Fair Employment Practices Act to guarantee 17 weeks' leave for all women with 1 year's service in organizations under federal jurisdiction. It also prohibited dismissal during the leave period, and guaranteed the same or comparable work on return.

Today, then, CBC women are governed by both federal law and CBC policy. The law guarantees them, after a 2-week waiting period with no pay, two-thirds of their maximum pensionable earnings (that is, two-thirds of up to $170 per week, or a maximum gross payment of $113 before taxes). In order to qualify for the full 15 weeks' payment, however, the woman must leave 10 weeks before the projected date of the birth. This gives her 2 weeks without pay; she can then collect benefits for 8 weeks before the birth, 1 week during confinement, and 6 weeks afterwards.*

Under CBC regulations, a woman may take up to 18 weeks without pay after 1 year's service. She may also prepay some benefits (Group Life and medical insurance, but not pension), but if she chooses to do so she must pay the Corporation's share of these costs as well as her own. If she wishes, and her

---

* Since the conclusion of our study, legislation has been introduced in Parliament which would make the 15-week period flexible; i.e., all 15 weeks could be taken during and after confinement. It is probable that this legislation will be passed during the current session.

EXAMPLE

It treats men the same as women . . .   . . . and avoids compromising special leave

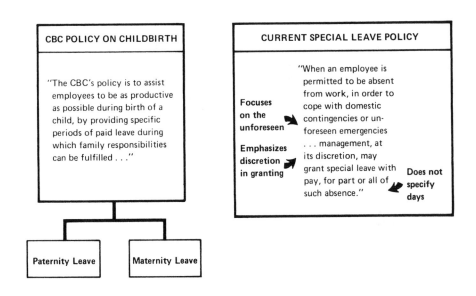

CBC POLICY ON CHILDBIRTH

"The CBC's policy is to assist employees to be as productive as possible during birth of a child, by providing specific periods of paid leave during which family responsibilities can be fulfilled . . ."

Paternity Leave   Maternity Leave

CURRENT SPECIAL LEAVE POLICY

Focuses on the unforeseen

Emphasizes discretion in granting

"When an employee is permitted to be absent from work, in order to cope with domestic contingencies or unforeseen emergencies . . . management, at its discretion, may grant special leave with pay, for part or all of such absence."

Does not specify days

Fig. 85 Separating Paternity from Special Leave has two main advantages

143

doctor agrees in writing, she may work right up to the time of birth. She is assured of her former position or of its equivalent - that is, a job in the same salary classification (Figure 86).

While the federal legislation and CBC policy together provide a much better situation than existed prior to 1970, individual women and the Corporation still face some problems. These range from financial and psychological troubles to effects on productivity.

Problems With Current Situation

Although it is commonly assumed that a woman having a baby has a man to help her with finances, it is important to emphasize that this is not always the case. The woman may be unmarried, and planning to have and raise a child on her own - a situation that is becoming more common each year. If she is married, as most are, she may well be providing the family's main income; in their 20s and early 30s, many women work while their husbands are studying. Or, though both are working, family finances may already be strained. Whether or not *"parenthood is something you plan - or should plan"*, as we were told many times, it does not always happen that way, and it is not always possible to make provision in advance for such events.

As things stand now, a woman suffers a reduction in income of at least one-third and possibly as much as 70 to 80 percent during maternity leave (Figure 87). And her income drops just when her expenses are likely to rise. As well as the overall reduction, there are interruptions in the "cash flow"; that is to say, there are breaks in the regularity of pay, which often make it difficult to keep up with the payment of fixed expenses.

The inflexibility of current unemployment insurance provisions compounds the problem. The woman cannot apply for unemployment insurance benefits until she has been off the CBC payroll for 2 weeks, and obtains a letter to that effect, together with a certificate of pregnancy from her doctor. Payments stop 6 weeks after the estimated date of the birth, whether or not the baby arrives on schedule. If she is not ready to go back to work at that time, she is out of income again. Some examples show how this works.

1. A healthy young woman who has never felt better may choose to continue with her job up to the time of delivery; if she does so, she will only be entitled to benefits from the date on which she is able to apply for them, having been unpaid for 2 weeks, and she cannot claim for more than 6 weeks following the week of confinement. This may mean she will receive unemployment insurance benefits for only 4 or 5 weeks, and if she chooses to take the 18 weeks allowed for by the CBC, the rest will be without income.

2. Another woman, equally healthy and willing to work, stops 10 weeks ahead of the projected birth date, so that she can take advantage of partial pay for all but 2 weeks of the CBC leave entitlement. The CBC is then losing her services at a time when she is quite willing and able to work, and may find that she returns reluctantly and often with

144

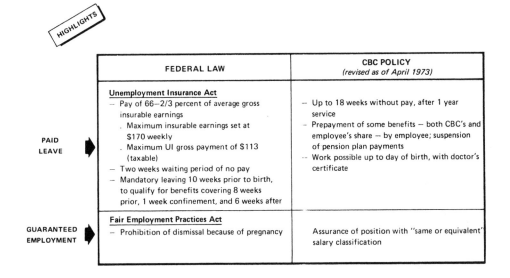

	FEDERAL LAW	CBC POLICY *(revised as of April 1973)*

PAID LEAVE	**Unemployment Insurance Act**
	— Pay of 66—2/3 percent of average gross insurable earnings
	  . Maximum insurable earnings set at $170 weekly
	  . Maximum UI gross payment of $113 (taxable)
	— Two weeks waiting period of no pay
	— Mandatory leaving 10 weeks prior to birth, to qualify for benefits covering 8 weeks prior, 1 week confinement, and 6 weeks after
		— Up to 18 weeks without pay, after 1 year service
		— Prepayment of some benefits — both CBC's and employee's share — by employee; suspension of pension plan payments
		— Work possible up to day of birth, with doctor's certificate

GUARANTEED EMPLOYMENT	**Fair Employment Practices Act** — Prohibition of dismissal because of pregnancy	Assurance of position with "same or equivalent" salary classification

Fig. 86 CBC Women are governed by federal law and Corporation policy

145

The income of the lower
paid woman is cut by
one-third . . .

. . . and the higher the
salary, the greater the
loss

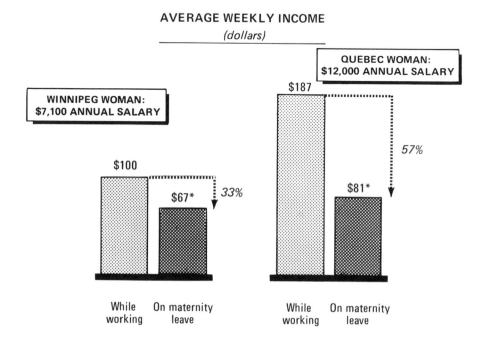

AVERAGE WEEKLY INCOME
(dollars)

QUEBEC WOMAN:
$12,000 ANNUAL SALARY

WINNIPEG WOMAN:
$7,100 ANNUAL SALARY

$187

$100

$67*   33%

$81*   57%

While
working

On maternity
leave

While
working

On maternity
leave

* — *Calculation based on:*
- *. 66-2/3% UIC pay less taxes*
- *. 2 weeks' waiting period with no pay*
- *. Prepayment of benefits*
- *. Maximum insurable earnings of $170 weekly*

Fig. 87   During maternity leave, a woman suffers a major income reduction

146

feelings of guilt at leaving a very young infant, 6 weeks after the birth. In such a case, both the woman - who would have preferred extra time with her child - and the CBC, which loses her when she is in good health and gets her back when she may need to be at home, are the losers.

3. The most unfortunate situation for both employer and employee arises when the baby is not cooperative, and refuses to be born on the date predicted. Since the benefits intended for the 6 weeks following the birth are being used up before and during confinement, the mother may have to return to work within 3 or 4 weeks of the birth, and may not be emotionally or physically ready to do so.

It is clear, then, that the inflexibility of the unemployment insurance process is at odds with the intent of both the legislation and the CBC regulations, and that both employees and Corporation suffer as a result.

A further complaint voiced by several women had to do with the red tape involved in making application for UIC payments. A few women told us they had been required to go to the local Manpower office and fill in forms indicating what kind of work they were looking for - although such a requirement is clearly not in line with policies set forth by the Unemployment Insurance Commission.

Perhaps the worst consequence of the present maternity leave system is that women who must cope with it often feel they are no longer regarded as serious employees (Figure 88), and think of themselves as being penalized in their careers because they are the childbearing sex. Although an ever-increasing number of women do and in many cases must work for the greater part of their adult lives, they point out that men may choose to be parents without making the sacrifices demanded of women.

The feeling of being valued less as an employee is made worse by the long-term financial losses a woman may suffer as a result of maternity. A career woman who has three children during her service with the CBC may lose a significant percentage of her pension (Figure 89), and might also suffer up to a 6-percent reduction in pension disability payments, should she ever be so unfortunate as to need them.

Outside Practice

What do other employers do to assist women in reconciling maternity with a career? In Canada, there appears to be little evidence that either industry or the Public Service has found solutions to the problem. Most private companies, as well as the Public Service, simply conform to the legal requirements, though a few enterprises such as the Bank of Montreal and Bell Canada do pay both the employees' and the employer's share of benefit costs for the leave period. The Canadian labour movement, however, is taking an increasingly aggressive stance; a resolution passed at the May 1974 meeting of the Canadian Labour Congress reads, in part: *"Be it resolved that the Canadian Labour Congress adopt a program . . . to*

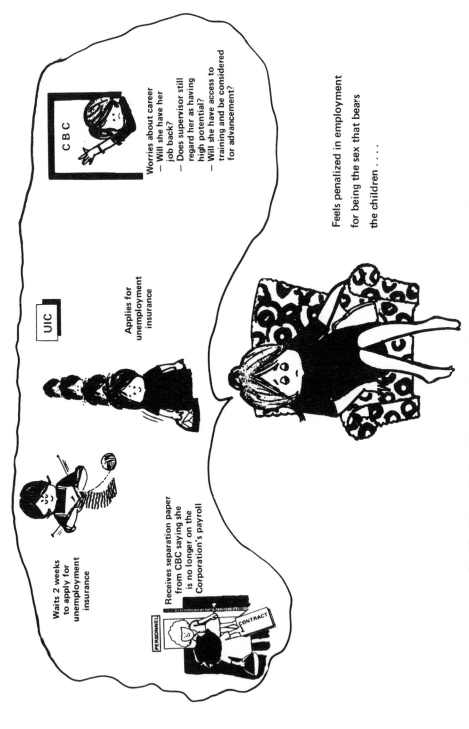

CBC

Worries about career
 — Will she have her
   job back?
 — Does supervisor still
   regard her as having
   high potential?
 — Will she have access to
   training and be considered
   for advancement?

Feels penalized in employment
for being the sex that bears
the children . . . . .

UIC

Applies for
unemployment
insurance

Waits 2 weeks
to apply for
unemployment
insurance

PERSONNEL

CONTRACT

Receives separation paper
from CBC saying she
is no longer on the
Corporation's payroll

Fig. 88   Women believe they are not regarded as serious career employees

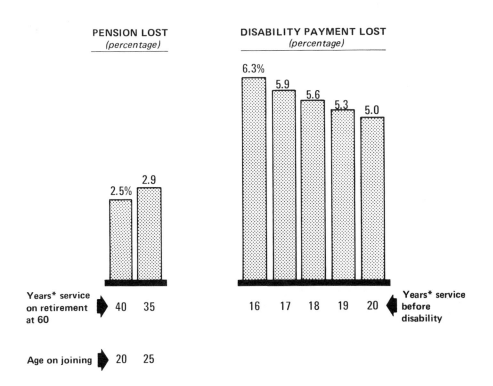

IMPACT: LOSS OF ONE YEAR'S PENSIONABLE SERVICE*

PENSION LOST
(percentage)

2.5% 2.9

Years* service on retirement at 60 ▶ 40 35

Age on joining ▶ 20 25

DISABILITY PAYMENT LOST
(percentage)

6.3% 5.9 5.6 5.3 5.0

16 17 18 19 20 ◀ Years* service before disability

* — *Assumes three children born while employee on CBC maternity leave without pay*

Fig. 89 A career woman with three "CBC children" can lose a noticeable percentage of pension and disability payments

establish maternity leave with full pay and benefits as right . . .". Member unions were asked to give priority to this resolution, seeking implementation in their various contractual agreements.

In the United States, where maternity leave is not covered by unemployment insurance, much more action is being taken. The proportion of women covered by company paid leave has doubled in the past 4 years, and now stands at 26 percent. Recent court cases also suggest that employers with disability plans may have no choice in the future; while many actions are still pending, the decisions so far have tended to classify maternity as a "temporary disability", to be covered under the normal plan.

Recommendations

Considering the many real problems CBC women face under the present system, the Task Force recommends that the Corporation:

> **38. Pay, for women with a minimum of 1 year's service, full salary and the Corporation's share of benefit costs during maternity leave for a period of up to 15 weeks, to be taken at her discretion, provided she signifies her intention to return.**

In evaluating alternative recommendations, our main concern was to balance out cost to the CBC and effectiveness in solving the problems caused by the present system (Figure 90). There are four possible alternatives. The first is for the CBC to make a small symbolic gesture, by paying both the Corporation's and the employee's share of benefit costs during the leave period. A second is the application of sick leave, and a third is to establish maternity leave benefits on the basis of "earning" a month of maternity leave per year up to a maximum of 15 weeks. The fourth is simply to pay full salary and the Corporation's share of benefits for 15 weeks, for an employee with 1 year's service.

We chose the fully paid leave because it is the *only* alternative that will eliminate the problems that now exist. Paying benefit costs would only meet about 10 percent of the income loss, while the disadvantages arising from the inflexibility and bureaucratic bother of unemployment insurance would remain. To apply sick leave would mean that a woman would have to wait 6 or 8 years before she earned enough credits to cover 15 weeks, provided she had never been sick; she would then be left with no credits to cover future illness. And allowing women to accumulate maternity leave credits at the rate of 4 weeks per year to a maximum of 15 weeks would still result in income loss for women with less than 3-3/4 years' service.

The remaining alternative is full payment. This would not only maintain the employee in the same income position as when she is at work - as the CBC now does for employees suffering from heart attacks, ulcers, and alcoholism - but also has the great advantage of removing the necessity of using the unemployment insurance system, with its rigidities, red tape, and suggestion of welfare.

ALTERNATIVES CONSIDERED

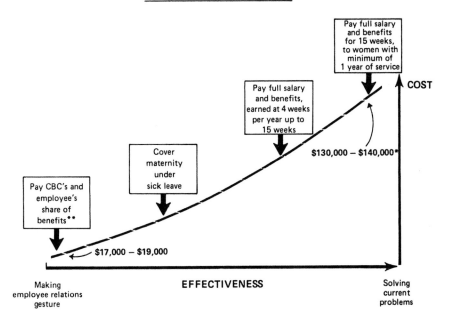

Fig. 90   In evaluating alternatives, the Task Force was concerned with balancing
cost and effectiveness

Beyond the cost and effectiveness factors, there were both advantages and disadvantages in the full pay formula.

Among the disadvantages was the disapproval of those who so vocally opposed any such move. It could also be argued that it is an economic waste for the CBC to pay an employee who could recover even part of her salary through unemployment insurance*. And many people worried about the danger that a woman might not return to work, despite her stated intention, leaving the CBC out of pocket. Finally, some felt that the numbers of employees affected in any one year by this new benefit would be very small, and that the resources available should go to matters affecting larger numbers of staff.

Having weighed all these arguments, we nevertheless believe that the benefits of fully paid leave are too important to be overlooked (Figure 91). Action of this kind would indicate a clear and real commitment to equal opportunity within the Corporation. It would also mean meeting the strongly expressed wish of a large number of employees - including nearly all employees in Montreal's French Services Division, and about half of all those we spoke to in other locations. As for the likelihood that women would not return as promised, we believe the number of people who might behave in this fashion would be extremely small; for one thing, even if they do not wish to return immediately, most young women now expect to reenter the work force at some future time, and would not be anxious to have such evidence on their records. There may indeed be few people affected in any one year; but over a period, they would add up to a sizeable proportion of the younger female staff.

If our recommendation in this matter is accepted, the CBC will be in a position of visible leadership in Canada. Politically, this may be difficult for the Corporation; it would be striking out on its own to give its female employees a better deal - with public funds - than that enjoyed by other women in the country. We believe, however, that it is in just such matters that the CBC as an enlightened employer should be setting the pace; it should not wait for union pressure and the example of others.

The Task Force's second recommendation related to maternity leave is that the CBC should:

39. Guarantee the new mother the identical position upon her return.

This recommendation is much more clear-cut. The advantages are significant, while the disadvantages are minor. Knowing that she can pick up her work where she left off, the employee will see that her career need not suffer

---

* Several people had suggested that CBC simply "make up the difference"; this we understand to be impossible under present legislation, which does not allow payment of any unemployment insurance funds to anyone receiving payment from an employer. Should the CBC be able to influence the Government to alter this legislation, another alternative would arise.

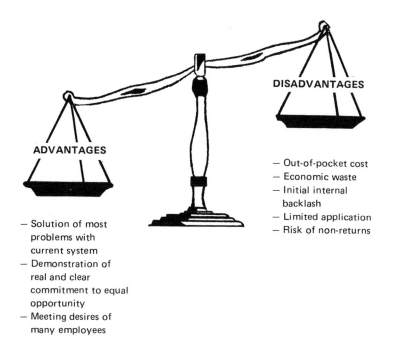

ADVANTAGES

DISADVANTAGES

— Solution of most
problems with
current system
— Demonstration of
real and clear
commitment to equal
opportunity
— Meeting desires of
many employees

— Out-of-pocket cost
— Economic waste
— Initial internal
backlash
— Limited application
— Risk of non-returns

Fig. 91   The benefits of fully paid leave outweigh the disadvantages

a break. This knowledge will go far to provide psychological assurance that the CBC and her supervisor are committed to her as a valuable employee. It will also prevent any supervisor from using maternity leave as a pretext for moving to another department an employee whom he or she does not want. Should the employee by any chance change her mind and not return, any inconvenience caused the department, such as the delay in finding a permanent replacement, would be no greater than the inconvenience caused by long illnesses. By "identical", we mean just that - *the same job.* This recommendation is intended to protect career aspirations as well as income level, by ensuring that, for example, a clerk who had been working for advancement in one department was not moved to what she saw as a dead-end job in another. However, it is obvious that the same *assignment* cannot always be guaranteed; a script assistant, for example, might not be able to return to the same series, as a change in mid-season might be damaging to the program.

CHILD CARE

Children, once born, must be cared for. In deciding what the Corporation's role, if any, should be in providing assistance to its employees in this area, the Task Force looked both at hard data and at opinions and attitudes. To gain the proper perspective on the problem, we first examined the overall need for child care in Canada, and the extent to which it is currently provided. We looked at the impact of the present situation on CBC staff, and on the Corporation, and we found what action employees thought the Corporation should take. We also examined what some other organizations were doing to help their employees, before we reached recommendations about the Corporation's role.

Situation in Canada

In this country, over half a million children under the age of 6 need care, either because both parents are working or because they have only one parent, who must either work or go on welfare. Only a fraction of this need has been met in the past. A 1967 study found that 97 percent of working mothers had no access to child care facilities. Another study in 1972 found that, of children under 6 whose mothers work, only 2 percent were accommodated in such centres (Figure 92). While almost everyone seems to agree that governments bear the primary responsibility for providing such facilities, little of real impact has been accomplished. The Federal Government provides subsidies to the provinces; they in turn usually make cost-sharing arrangements with municipalities, which either operate centres directly, or subsidize facilities set up by community groups. But centres set up under this arrangement are few in comparison with the need, and the gap between the demand and the availability of care seems to be widening (Figure 93).

Nor is there much hope that private enterprise will respond to the need, since providing child care is not a profitable proposition. On the revenue side of the equation, government subsidies are limited, and apply only to children of low-income parents. On the cost side, it is impossible to cut

Study* in 1967 showed 97 percent of working mothers had no access to child care facilities . . .

. . . and 5 years later, less than 2 percent of children under six were enrolled in child care facilities

WORKING
MOTHERS
(percentage: 1972)

CHILDREN UNDER
SIX WITH
WORKING PARENTS
(1972)

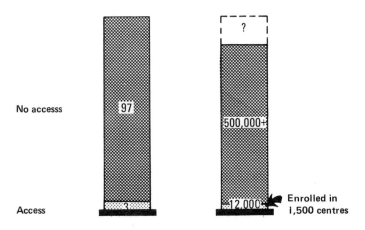

No accesss

97

?

500,000+

Access

2

12,000

Enrolled in
1,500 centres

*   —   *By Canadian Council for Social Development*

Fig. 92   Child care provision in no way matches demand

PATTERN OF GOVERNMENT ACTION
ON CHILD CARE

Federal
Government
provides
subsidies
under
Canada
Assistance
Plan . . .

. . . to the
Provinces*,
which
typically
enter cost-
sharing
arrangements
with
municipalities . . .

. . . which
operate
their own
or subsidize
others . . .

. . . but this
action has
not closed
the gap

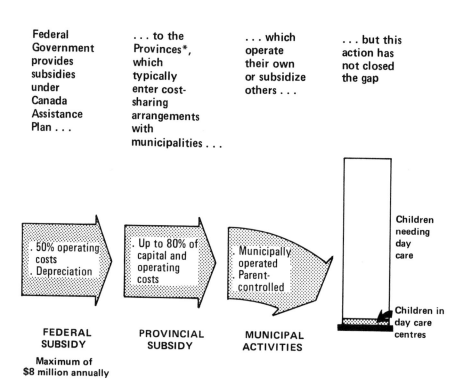

. 50% operating
  costs
. Depreciation

. Up to 80% of
  capital and
  operating
  costs

. Municipally
  operated
. Parent-
  controlled

Children
needing
day
care

Children in
day care
centres

FEDERAL
SUBSIDY

PROVINCIAL
SUBSIDY

MUNICIPAL
ACTIVITIES

Maximum of
$8 million annually

* — *Only for the few provinces with day nursery legislation —*
    e.g., Ontario, British Columbia

Fig. 93   Federal and provincial actions have had little impact

corners to any great extent. Most provinces and municipalities have strict regulations concerning the numbers and qualifications of staff. Fire and health standards are also naturally high, and facilities are closely scrutinized. In short, child care is expensive to provide, but most of the families that require it, though not classed as "low-income", cannot afford to pay actual costs - and certainly not the higher fees that would allow the operators to make a profit.

The resulting situation is highly unsatisfactory in most communities. The scarcity of facilities creates real problems for the family, and often for employers as well. Parents are often restricted in the kind of work they can take, though they may need and want to build a career. A single mother who has to stay home and resort to welfare until her children are in school frequently finds it hard to get back into the work force, just at the time when her children's education, food, clothing, and shelter are most expensive. The longer she stays at home, the poorer her chances of ever getting a job that pays a decent salary. Or, if she does manage to work, her employer may suffer: she may be reluctant to take on overtime or shift work, or to be away from the phone for more than a few minutes during the day; she may be absent too often because of the undependable arrangements she has had to make. In short, an employee is almost certain to be less productive when worrying about the kind of care the children are getting.

Problems in the CBC

Not surprisingly, the general situation in Canada is reflected in the CBC. Over and over again, women told us of their difficulties in getting adequate care for their children; many had to spend far more than they could really afford in order to get proper care (Figure 94), while others settled for unsatisfactory stopgap arrangements. We also heard from supervisors who were convinced that better child care would make some of their employees more productive. Although facts and figures were not available, interviews and discussions convinced us that these problems affect a large number of employees. In almost every group interview, there was at least one single parent - usually female, but sometimes male. Many of the married mothers work because they have to; some of their husbands are at university, and some are incapacitated or unemployed. In many other cases, even with the husband's salary, another income is needed to bring the family up to an acceptable living standard. Others work in order to establish a career in a field where they believe they have something to offer.

Most of these parents are dissatisfied with the arrangements they have been forced to make, either because of the cost, or because they are unreliable or inflexible. Many hire baby-sitters, who may let the children sit in front of the TV set all day. And the sitters sometimes come late or are sick - forcing the mother to be late or absent herself. A number take their children to private homes, where conditions vary. Often these homes belong to low-income families, which need the money, but where the woman has no professional training in caring for children. Only a very few CBC employees have access to licensed child care centres. The availability of both baby-sitters and private homes often varies from month to month, and the recur-

COMPARISON OF "DISPOSABLE" INCOME FOR
CUPE O & P CLERK 3*

With one preschooler:

ALTERNATIVE # 1:
Welfare

ALTERNATIVE # 2:
Work and Child Care

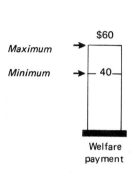

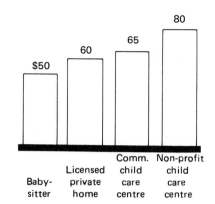

With two preschoolers:

ALTERNATIVE # 1:
Welfare

ALTERNATIVE # 2:
Work and Child Care

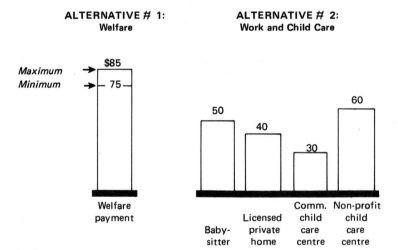

* — *Average income = $100 per week*
Average "disposable" income = $(100 − cost of child care)

Fig. 94   Child care is so expensive that low-income employees might be better off on welfare

curing search for adequate arrangements puts a severe strain on both the emotions and the energy of many women.

Even the few who use child care centres run into problems resulting from the inflexibility of the centre's regulations or its location. Most centres close by 6:00 p.m., so shift work and overtime are impossible for the parent. The majority do not accept children under the age of 2, so that women with more than one child often have to make two sets of arrangements. Some must leave home very early in the mornings to make two "deliveries", and repeat the trip at 5:00 p.m. The round trip is sometimes excessively long.

This situation is unquestionably hard on the employees concerned; but it seems clear that it also affects the CBC adversely. It is hard to assign work fairly if certain employees cannot acccept shift work or overtime; the un-avoidable absences when baby-sitters do not turn up are certainly disrupt-ive; and productivity must obviously suffer when parents are worrying about their children instead of their work, or travelling such great distances that their energies are sapped.

The Task Force had also to consider other questions. How much respons-ibility do employees think the CBC should take in solving the problem? What do other organizations do in the same circumstances? And what recommendations could we make, considering that we did not have time to measure precisely the extent of the need, or to estimate the practicality and costs of various solutions?

Whose Responsibility?

There is one point on which almost all employees do agree: governments are not fulfilling their role in answering a countrywide need. And very few expect the situation to improve in the near future. But agreement ends there. Across Canada, roughly half of the staff feel strongly that the CBC should take some action. They see such action as *"affording the only hope of meeting the needs"*, or say it *"permits the mother and the single parents to work more effectively day by day"*, *"enables women to pursue a career"*, and would *"improve the productivity of the Corporation"*. The other half, for a variety of reasons, firmly believe that the CBC should stay out of the child care business. It *"takes money away from programs"*, *"adds unnecessary administrative problems"*, *"pushes paternalism too far"*, *"subsidizes people with children; why not those with parents to care for?"*. We found that opinion divided to some extent by location. Staff in French Services in Montreal were almost unanimous in supporting CBC action; in other centres, the split was often about even.

A number of non-governmental organizations are now providing their em-ployees with child care assistance. In Toronto, Riverdale Hospital has child care facilities on its premises; the employees pay a fee, but the hospital subsidizes the centre as well. McMaster University is in the process of starting a centre. There, the parents, helped by provincial/municipal sub-sidies, pay the operating costs, but pay no rent as the space is provided free by the University. The federal Public Service has also been considering the possibility of assisting its employees, and has done a good deal of ground-work in the Ottawa-Hull area. It has conducted a thorough survey of the needs of its employees, and is drawing up a master plan to meet them. The Department of Public Works has developed its own blueprint for a specific project for the children of its staff members (Figure 95), and theTreasury Board is in the process of formulating Government policy on the subject.

In the United States, companies that have assisted employees report good results. There, the aid has taken several forms; some small firms have set up their own centres; others contribute to community programs, and still others subsidize centres run by unions. Whatever the specific plan, these firms generally claim that they have benefited significantly, with improved re-cruitment, lower absenteeism, greater productivity, and better employee relations.

We return then to the question: whose responsibility is the care of em-ployees' small children? Although many people believe that governments at some or all levels should undertake to provide it, as they provide for schooling when children are older, government assistance is not likely to answer the need in the foreseeable future. Some people believe that child care is solely the responsibility of the parents; but many parents cannot afford proper care, and its lack affects not only themselves and their child-ren, but their work. The only avenue for solving the immediate problem seems to be through action by the CBC; so whether or not it ought to be the employer's responsibility, the Task Force saw no alternative.

And from the evidence alone, the CBC would benefit from taking action. Before proposing a specific solution for the Corporation, however, we felt that some additional questions needed to be answered. First, the extent of employee demand must be measured. Exactly how many employees do need child care assistance, and where are they? What arrangements does each of these employees have now? Under what financial and other circumstances would they use CBC-assisted facilities? Second, the nature of the CBC's involvement should be decided upon. What are the basic alternatives for aiding employees, given the size and the nature of the demand? How much subsidy would the Corporation need to provide to have a real impact on the problem? If employees in one location were assisted, must those in other centres be helped too? Finally, the practical implications of any action must be considered. Exactly what costs would be involved? Can the CBC provide space "on site"? How should a child care program be administered, and by whom? What is the legal responsibility of running a centre?

Recommendations

In summary, then, the main conclusions of the Task Force concerning child care were these. The lack of good child care facilities prevents a significant number of CBC employees, primarily women, from enjoying equal opportun-

PILOT DAY CARE CENTRE

To provide for 25 children between the ages of 2-1/2 to 5
between the hours of 8 a.m. to 6 p.m. (5 days per week)

Capital Cost

Portable classroom with washrooms — $11,000 purchase, or
$375 monthly rent, with option to purchase

Operating Statement

Costs	Year 1	Year 2
Rent	$ 4,500	$ 4,500
Salaries	8,500	9,000
	6,000	6,500
	6,000	6,300
	6,000	6,200
Supply teacher at $2.50/hour	1,500	1,500
Equipment	5,000	nil
Food	4,000	4,000
Liability insurance	60	60
Office expense (health supplies, telephone)	500	500
	$42,060	$38,560
Income		
— Subsidies and pay from parents ($7.32 daily)	$42,750	$42,750
PROFIT	$ 690	$ 4,190

Profit to be reinvested into DCC

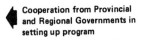

Cooperation from Provincial
and Regional Governments in
setting up program

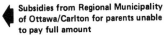

Subsidies from Regional Municipality
of Ottawa/Carlton for parents unable
to pay full amount

*Fig. 95   The budget for the day care centre being considered by the Public
Works Department is relatively modest*

ity in work, and also makes them less productive as employees of the Corporation. It is the responsibility of governments to improve the situation for everyone, but it is not likely that government action will make much impact within the foreseeable future. Roughly half of CBC employees believe that the CBC, as a good employer, should help to fill the gap, and there is an embryonic trend for other employers to take this kind of action. Finally, a number of crucial questions concerning the CBC's involvement have yet to be answered.

Against this background, the Task Force recommends that the Corporation:

40. Undertake to provide assistance to employees in obtaining improved child care facilities.

41. Undertake, as a first step, a feasibility study in Montreal to determine what form the assistance should take.

The feasibility study should be carried out by the Office of Equal Opportunity, and its objectives should be fourfold:

1.   Determine the extent and nature of employee demand in Montreal.

2.   Map out alternatives for CBC assistance - e.g., cooperation with outside agencies; free space only; fully subsidized centre.

3.   Assess the practical implications of each alternative.

4.   Recommend a national CBC policy, and a specific action program.

The initial work should focus on Montreal, since it is the area where the greatest need was expressed, and where there was near unanimity that action ought to be taken.

Having concluded that problems associated with parenthood prevent many CBC women from achieving equality of opportunity, the Task Force feels strongly that the Corporation should take positive steps to minimize the effects of these problems. Recommended steps include the initiation of a childbirth policy, which would entitle employees to paid paternity leave (3 days) and paid maternity leave (15 weeks). A woman taking maternity leave would also be guaranteed the same position on her return. The Task Force also recommended that the CBC should find means to assist their employees with obtaining satisfactory child care, and as a first step it should undertake a feasibility study in Montreal with a view to establishing a child care centre there as a pilot project.

This chapter concludes our analysis of the problems women face in achieving equal opportunity in the CBC. We shall next consider how the CBC should go about implementing the program we have recommended.

MANAGEMENT RESPONSE

The Task Force has made six recommendations dealing with the responsibilities of parenthood. Management is generally in agreement with their
direction and underlying rationale. However, we have some reservations
about a number of specific details which are described below.

Paternity Leave

36. **Establish, for employees with 1 year of service or
    more, a separate paid paternity leave, to be included in an
    overall birth policy.**
    Accepted in full.

37. **Set the leave entitlement at 3 days.**
    Accepted in full.

Maternity Leave

38. **Pay, for women with a minimum of 1 year's service,
    full salary and the Corporation's share of benefit costs
    during maternity leave for a period of up to 15 weeks,
    to be taken at her discretion, provided she signifies her
    intention to return.**
    Principle of some level of paid leave accepted; fully paid
    leave not accepted. In our view, the Task Force has made
    a thorough and balanced analysis of the advantages
    and disadvantages of paid maternity leave. Further, we
    fully understand why the group - operating from its
    mandate of ensuring equal opportunity for women - has
    concluded that fully paid leave is the only complete
    answer to the many problems created by the current
    combination of federal legislation and CBC policy. How-
    ever, from our perspective, only a more modest level of
    reimbursement is appropriate.

    Specifically, the Task Force has pointed out that the lead-
    ing companies in Canada pay maternity leave only to the
    extent of the employee's and organization's share of
    benefits. Clearly, then, adoption of fully paid leave
    would put the CBC far ahead of any large private or
    public corporation in the country.

    As a first step, therefore, the Corporation accepts the
    recommendation to pay both the employee's and the
    Corporation's share of the cost of benefits during
    maternity leave. Beyond this, the Corporation must re-
    serve its decision. The Task Force has made an excellent
    case for fully paid leave; but since its work was com-
    pleted, the federal government has introduced amend-
    ments to the portion of the unemployment insurance
    legislation that governs maternity payments. Thus, we

wish to reserve our decision on the Task Force's recommendation until the fate of those amendments is clear.

39. Guarantee the new mother the identical position upon her return.
Accepted, subject to further clarification of the ground rules for application. The intent of this recommendation is clear and is one that management fully supports. However, we believe that more specific operational definitions are needed. For example, does "identical" mean *the* same position in the same organization unit in the same location, or - alternatively - could a senior clerk in accounting at Head Office be transferred to a senior clerk accounting position with the same duties and same salary, but in the Ottawa Area?

As we see it, this and similar questions should be answered both to provide an unambiguous policy which prevents misunderstanding, and to define fully the extent of the Corporation's flexibility in balancing work loads and finding staff replacements when a woman is absent for the 18 weeks of maternity leave. Thus, we accept the Task Force's recommendation, but reserve the opportunity to approve ground rules for its specific application.

Child Care

40. Undertake to provide assistance to employees in obtaining improved child care facilities.

41. Undertake, as a first step, a feasibility study in Montreal to determine what form the assistance should take.
Both recommendations accepted in part. We believe it inappropriate to make a commitment in this complex area without first knowing the answers to the many questions the Task Force identifies as still unanswered in the preceding pages of this chapter. However, we agree that a feasibility study in Montreal is an excellent way to obtain these answers, as well as to move positively in the direction of assisting employees there - should the project conclude that such assistance is both feasible and desirable.

Thus, we agree to:

- **Undertake a Montreal feasibility study, part of whose mandate is to recommend a corporate-wide policy and approach to child care.**

- Determine *upon completion* of the study whether the CBC should make a firm commitment to assist in this area, and the various forms that assistance will take across Canada.

7. OVERALL ACTION PROGRAM

In the previous chapters, we have described the barriers standing in the way of equal opportunity for women in the CBC, and recommended 41 actions that we believe would together eliminate them. It might be thought that this was the end of the work of the Task Force.

But to stop at this point would mean leaving the job half finished. Since our recommendations are many, diverse, and sometimes complex, we felt it essential to work out the means for putting them into effect. In order to do so, we had first to organize the recommendations into a comprehensive action program. We then had to determine how the requirements for full implementation could be met: what staff support would be needed, the kind of management involvement that would be necessary, and ways to hold managers accountable (Figure 96).

THE EQUAL OPPORTUNITY PROGRAM

Looking over the recommendations, it is apparent that they all fall into one of three categories: policies, administrative mechanisms, or training to change attitudes. The third category gets at the root cause of most of the present problems - that is, the stereotyped view that many CBC men have of women - and clearly, work must be started immediately in this area. Changing attitudes is always a slow process, and cannot be accomplished through training alone. In the meantime, however, as we pointed out in the chapter on job access, it is urgent that behaviour be altered, both in order to assure just treatment of all employees, and to provide "models of success", which in themselves are among the most effective agents for change. This requires a simultaneous attack through policies, which make very clear where the CBC stands, and changes in existing practices in a number of areas. As policy statements and new systems succeed in breaking down existing barriers, the resulting change in the kinds of jobs women hold should encourage the skeptical to reexamine old assumptions.

An example might best show how policies, mechanisms, and training will complement each other. A policy prohibiting supervisors from turning down qualified applicants on the basis of sex is a step towards hiring women for "men's jobs". The addition of two mechanisms - provision of a list of qualified women candidates and the use of selection boards - will help to ensure that women get into positions from which they have traditionally been barred. If they then succeed in showing that they can do these jobs, it is hoped supervisors will begin to question their own attitudes and change their views. This first-hand experience should also be reinforced by awareness sessions.

Although the attack must be made simultaneously along three fronts, it would be impossible to undertake all the many individual steps at the same

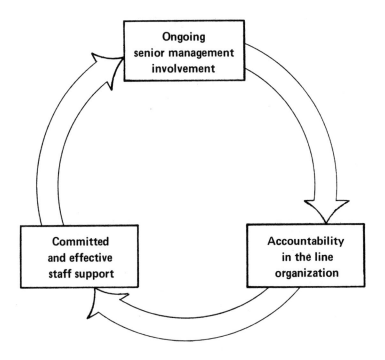

Fig. 96 There are three requirements for successful implementation of the action program

time. No organization can absorb a great many changes all at once, and even with total commitment, the CBC has neither the staff nor the financial resources to manage it. Furthermore, it will be necessary for the equal opportunity program to dovetail with the overall human resources improvement effort, and the department that must carry out that program is just now in the course of being restructured.

With these restraints in mind, the Task Force recommends that the CBC:

42. Undertake a long-term equal opportunity program, which would phase in the recommended changes over a period of 3 to 4 years.

In the short term, this program should demonstrate the CBC's commitment by achieving some specific and tangible results, primarily in the benefits area, within 9 months. Thereafter, it would place top priority on improving access to the full range of jobs for all CBC employees (Figure 97).

It is important to show immediate results in at least a few areas, if only because of the expectations of both employees and outside observers. As to where to start, it seemed logical to attack problems that affect a large number of women, and that are sufficiently clear-cut to allow immediate action to be taken. Obvious areas include the revision of policies and guidelines; the preparation of new recruitment materials; and the equalization of pension and group life insurance plans.

To develop the longer term and more complete plan, it was necessary to attach priorities to the individual problem areas. We rated individual areas on the basis of the number of women affected, the seriousness of the impact, and the depth of feeling expressed with relation to each (Figure 98). Lack of access to the majority of jobs, for example, affects almost the entire female staff, and also elicited an intense reaction from most women. Inequalities in pay, on the other hand, while universally deplored, affect only a minority of women - though these individuals feel a deep sense of injury. In rating problem areas in this way, we by no means suggest that those with lower ratings be ignored; the ratings are simply one element to be considered in determining priorities, so that scarce resources such as money and time can be properly allocated. Thus, for example, a problem affecting only a few women, such as the wording of Northern Allowances regulations, can be put right at the stroke of a pen, and would be dealt with immediately. The development of an evaluation system for secretaries, which affects a large number of women - and is also high on the list in terms of depth of feeling - would of necessity have to wait slightly longer because of the organization and financing that is required.

With these priorities, summarized in Figure 99, in mind, the program should see, by the end of its first year, the launching of a feasibility study on child care; the development of awareness sessions; and a start at improving basic processes in hiring and advancement. By the beginning of the second year, the two secretarial projects and a number of local affirmative action programs should be under way. By the end of 1977, along with the continuing programs, all locations should be beginning to benefit from the experi-

OVERVIEW OF EQUAL OPPORTUNITY PROGRAM

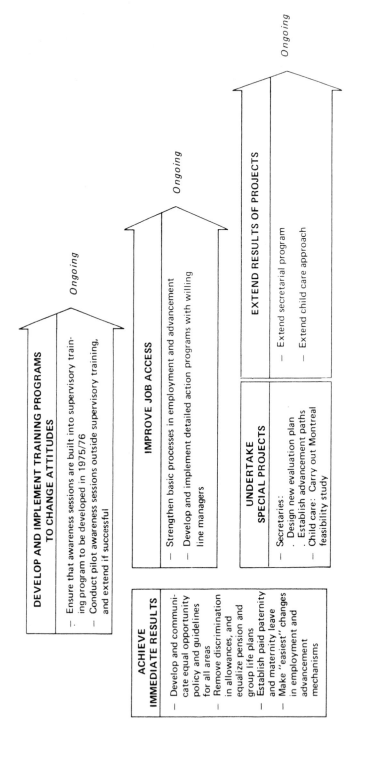

DEVELOP AND IMPLEMENT TRAINING PROGRAMS TO CHANGE ATTITUDES

Ongoing

- Ensure that awareness sessions are built into supervisory training program to be developed in 1975/76
- Conduct pilot awareness sessions outside supervisory training, and extend if successful

ACHIEVE IMMEDIATE RESULTS

- Develop and communicate equal opportunity policy and guidelines for all areas
- Remove discrimination in allowances, and equalize pension and group life plans
- Establish paid paternity and maternity leave
- Make "easiest" changes in employment and advancement mechanisms

IMPROVE JOB ACCESS

Ongoing

- Strengthen basic processes in employment and advancement
- Develop and implement detailed action programs with willing line managers

UNDERTAKE SPECIAL PROJECTS

- Secretaries:
  . Design new evaluation plan
  . Establish advancement paths
- Child care: Carry out Montreal feasibility study

EXTEND RESULTS OF PROJECTS

Ongoing

- Extend secretarial program
- Extend child care approach

Calendar year	1975	1976	1977	1978

Fig. 97   The Task Force recommends a 4-year, 5-part program

168

SUMMARY PROBLEM AREA		NEGATIVE IMPACT						DEPTH OF NEGATIVE FEELING						OVERALL SERIOUSNESS SCORE
		Number of Women Affected			Seriousness of Impact			Number of Women Unhappy			Intensity of Feeling			
	Points	Most (5)	Many (3)	Few (1)	High (5)	Medium (3)	Low (1)	Most (5)	Many (3)	Few (1)	High (5)	Medium (3)	Low (1)	
JOB ACCESS		▨			▨			▨			▨			20
SECRETARIES — Advancement			▨		▨			▨			▨			18
SECRETARIES — Rug Ranking			▨			▨		▨			▨			16
SECRETARIES — Treatment on the Job			▨		▨			▨			▨			18
COMPENSATION — Equal Pay for Equal Work				▨			▨			▨		▨		6
COMPENSATION — Group Life		▨				▨		▨				▨		16
COMPENSATION — Pension		▨					▨	▨				▨		14
COMPENSATION — Allowances				▨		▨			▨				▨	5
PARENTHOOD — Maternity Leave				▨		▨		▨				▨		10
PARENTHOOD — Child Care			▨		▨			▨			▨			14

Fig. 98 We rated problem areas by the number of women affected, the seriousness of the impact, and the depth of feeling expressed

SERIOUSNESS OF PROBLEMS

Most serious

AREA	POINTS
Limited job access	20
Advancement } Secretaries Treatment on the job }	18
Rug ranking	16
Group life	16
Pension	14
Child care	14
Maternity leave	10
Equal pay for equal work	6
Allowances	5

Less serious

Fig. 99   Job access is clearly the most serious problem

170

ence of individual pilot projects, as well as from the improved selection mechanisms and the awareness training sessions.

STAFF SUPPORT

We believe that this long-term attack on discrimination through policies, mechanisms, and training is a logical and practical one. We do, however, recognize that there are many difficulties involved in putting it into action. It requires a great deal of work; the secretarial project alone is both complicated and time-consuming. And there may be a tendency for momentum and commitment to drop over a period of time; bureaucracies resist change, and the cynicism arising from a history of less than successful task force endeavours is not helpful.

The fact is that the best-laid plans of mice and men - and certainly of task forces - are useless unless someone sees that they are put into practice. After months of intensive work, the members of this particular Task Force are determined that all the recommendations accepted by senior management should be acted upon.

To ensure the essential staff support for the program, the Task Force recommends that the Corporation:

43. **Create an Office of Equal Opportunity (OEO) and direct it to give top priority to implementing the program to ensure equal opportunity for women in the CBC.**

44. **Establish the following positions within the OEO, reporting to the senior human resources manager:**

   — **At the corporate level, a Director reporting to the Vice-President, Human Resources, and supported by two coordinators and a research analyst**

   — **In each division, an equal opportunity officer who reports to the Director, Human Resources**

   — **In each region, an equal opportunity representative, who may be full- or part-time, and who reports to the senior personnel officer.**

In deciding what form the staff support for the equal opportunity program should take, there were two main alternatives. The program could be made the responsibility of a strengthened human resources organization, or the CBC could create a separate office, which would carry out a number of tasks on its own, as well as working with the human resources staff to accomplish others.

While the choice was difficult, we chose the second option because we believed it would have some important advantages. First, it would provide the sheer manpower to get this complex job done - a very necessary provision, since even the strengthened human resources organization was not designed to handle this extra work load. Second, it would concentrate committed expertise on this specialized and extremely sensitive area; personnel with the required skills and convictions would be appointed with this specific job in mind. Third, it would provide a staff to monitor the entire program, and the means to coordinate its many elements. Moreover, a separate office would provide tangible evidence to all employees that the CBC is serious in its attempt to ensure equality of opportunity, and would meet a need identified by a number of women's groups. These advantages seemed to us to outweigh any fears that the setting up of such an office might create backlash, or might not be properly integrated with the rest of the human resources structures.

Once the Task Force decided that a separate office was required, there were numerous other questions to answer. What should be its basic mission, and what should it be called? What specific responsibilities should it have - and which should it not have? How should it be organized: to whom should it report, and how many people would be involved? Where would they be situated? Finally, how should the CBC go about staffing it? These questions are dealt with in the following pages.

Mission of the Office

An important aspect of the equal opportunity program is that, although it was designed primarily to ensure equality for women, implementation of most of its recommendations will benefit male staff as well. While the equalization of benefit plans, for example, applies exclusively to women, recommendations concerning paternity leave and the child care project, among others, will also directly affect a number of men. Still others, such as the establishment of selection boards, the improvement of employment practices, and the awareness sessions, will have long-term advantages to both sexes. Therefore, while we considered a "women's bureau" as an alternative, we concluded that the office should be called the Office of Equal Opportunity, and that its basic mission should be:

> "To ensure that all CBC employees enjoy equality of opportunity - without regard to sex, religion, age, marital status, or national origin - in all areas of employment within the Corporation".

The emphasis of the Office would probably change over a period of time (Figure 100). For the first 2 or 3 years, its major priority should be the implementation of the equal opportunity program recommended by the Task Force, and about 90 percent of its time and effort would be dedicated to that task. At the same time, it would have the responsibility of seeing that men do not suffer any discrimination.

To implement the equal opportunity program, the OEO would have to concern itself with eight kinds of tasks:

1. Developing comprehensive equal opportunity policies for all areas, and preparing guidelines to be followed in administering them.

172

OEO PRIORITIES
AND ALLOCATION OF EFFORT

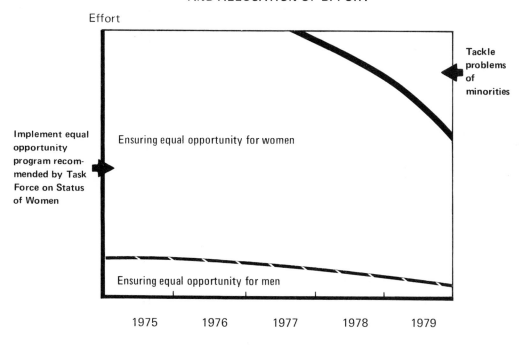

Fig. 100 *The emphasis of the Office of Equal Opportunity should change over time*

2. Undertaking specific projects that are outside the scope of the regular activities of the personnel department, such as carrying out a feasibility study on child care, and undertaking a project on secretarial career paths.

3. Ensuring that the strengthened human resources organization carries out its part, as in:

   Compensation: Equalizing the Pension and Group Life Plans, and establishing an evaluation plan for secretarial jobs

   Training: Ensuring that awareness sessions are built into supervisory training

   Manpower planning: Establishing selection boards, maintaining a list of high-potential women, and changing employment practices.

4. Working with line managers and unions to develop affirmative action programs.

5. Advising and counselling senior management on targets to be built into operating objectives.

6. Ensuring that issues concerning the status of women remain "visible" in the CBC, through a comprehensive publicity program.

7. Establishing collaborative relationships with CBC women's groups.

8. Monitoring the success of the overall program, and making periodic reports to both management and staff.

As is clear from these tasks, the OEO would concentrate mainly on programs affecting large sections of staff, rather than on the problems of individuals. A staff of the size we envisage would find it impossible to carry out this work if it were also called upon to investigate individual cases of apparent discrimination. Individual complaints do exist, and it would be unrealistic to expect that they will cease to arise. But it is our belief that they should be dealt with by a separate mechanism*. After the initial 2 or 3 years, it is hoped that the Office could tackle other problems, such as the lack of representation of minorities in certain CBC functions.

---

* *Our recommendation concerning the ombudsman function for the investigation of individual complaints is discussed in Appendix 1, together with other issues that affect all staff, or were not strictly within the Task Force's original mandate.*

Organizing the OEO

Given the decentralized nature of the CBC, it seemed important to establish an equal opportunity presence at each of the three major organizational levels of the Corporation. Two possible reporting channels were considered for the OEO at these three levels. The Office might report directly to senior line management; that is, to the President or Executive Vice-President at the corporate level, to the Vice-President - General Manager at the divisional level, and to the Regional Director at regional centres. Alternatively, the Office could be placed within the human resources organization, reporting to the Vice-President, Human Resources; the Director, Human Resources in the divisions; and the personnel managers in the regions.

While some of the women's groups recommended the first option, feeling that it would give the Office greater weight and visibility, the advantages were less persuasive than those of the second alternative. Specifically, by building the Office into the human resources organization, we believe that (1) the equal opportunity program would be more effectively integrated with overall personnel activities; (2) the Office would gain the active support and involvement of senior staff personnel; (3) working relationships between the Office and other human resources managers (training, compensation, etc.) would be made easier.

As well as their formal reporting lines at the three levels of management, the regional and divisional staff would have a strong working relationship with the Head Office OEO personnel (Figure 101). That Office would work with each level to establish policies and priorities to follow, but day-to-day decisions would be taken through the personnel line, thus adopting the system that is already used in many departments of the CBC.

For the first 2 or 3 years, the OEO would need about 10 full-time staff; five in Head Office, five elsewhere. The corporate office would be headed by a Director, with a secretary, two coordinators (who would act as project leaders for the action programs), and one research analyst. In each of the two major divisions, there would be a full-time equal opportunity officer; and in Engineering Headquarters, Special Services, and the regions, equal opportunity representatives, some of whom would be full-time, and some executing other functions as well. Full-time representatives would be required, for instance, in regions undertaking major action programs; a representative might spend a year in, say, Winnipeg or Halifax, and when the project was completed, move to another centre where a new one was planned.

It is difficult to estimate now the number of staff that would be needed, once the initial work is completed. Requirements would be dictated partly by the success of the Office in implementing programs; partly by the degree of its acceptance by both staff and management; and partly by the amount of work still to be done. If few projects remained to be carried out, the numbers might shrink. Ideally, the whole Office would work itself out of a job in a few years, and the remaining staff would be absorbed into the general human resources organization; in this imperfect world, however, we would hesitate to set a target date for the Office's demise. The Anti-Discrimination

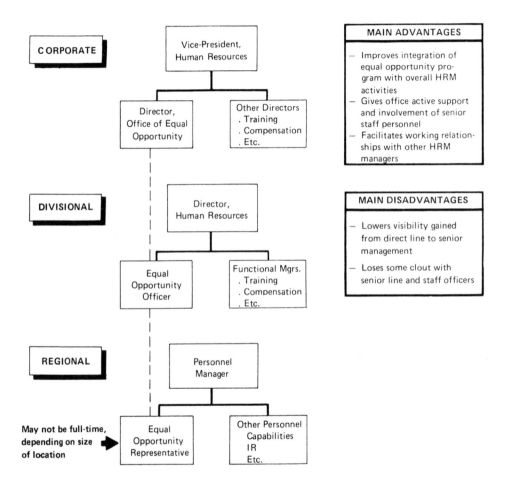

CORPORATE

Vice-President, Human Resources

Director, Office of Equal Opportunity

Other Directors
. Training
. Compensation
. Etc.

DIVISIONAL

Director, Human Resources

Equal Opportunity Officer

Functional Mgrs.
. Training
. Compensation
. Etc.

REGIONAL

Personnel Manager

Equal Opportunity Representative

Other Personnel Capabilities
IR
Etc.

May not be full-time, depending on size of location

MAIN ADVANTAGES
— Improves integration of equal opportunity program with overall HRM activities
— Gives office active support and involvement of senior staff personnel
— Facilitates working relationships with other HRM managers

MAIN DISADVANTAGES
— Lowers visibility gained from direct line to senior management
— Loses some clout with senior line and staff officers

Fig. 101   Regional and divisional OEO staff would report through the personnel line, but would have a strong working relationship with other levels of the OEO

Branch of the Public Service reports that only 20 percent of the complaints it receives are based on sexual discrimination; we suspect that the CBC may have more work to do along lines of which it is not yet even aware.

What kind of people should staff the Office, and how should they be recruited? The job is, admittedly, a difficult and complex one; the Office will be serving diverse, and often conflicting constituencies - management, women, men, minorities - and will have a heavy work load. The need for excellent relationships with those in charge of other human resources activities, and the problems of working within a highly decentralized organization, add to the demands of the undertaking. It is therefore clear that it will require a staff with unusual qualifications; they must, for example, be acceptable to and respected by all constituencies; be both firm and tactful; be committed to an equal opportunity program; and finally, be willing and able to travel extensively.

Because we consider the staffing of this Office of the utmost importance, the Task Force recommends that the Corporation:

45. Staff the OEO using the selection board process: Appoint the Director first, including the Task Force members on the selection board.

It goes without saying that we are strongly committed to the principle of selection boards, as a means to avoid any individual bias. We also believe that our own involvement in the process of selecting the Director provides a necessary link between our work and the implementation of our recommendations, as our familiarity with the program and knowledge of the background research puts us in a good position to judge the suitability of candidates. We think it important to make this appointment without delay, so that the Director can have a hand in the choice of the other staff for the Office.

MANAGEMENT INVOLVEMENT

Even with an office entirely staffed by the most effective and eager spirits, the equal opportunity program will fail without the full support and continuing involvement of senior management, including corporate and divisional officers and regional directors. This involvement is essential - first, to make clear to everyone that equal opportunity remains a corporate priority; second, to let down-the-line management know that real progress is expected; and third, to make sure that employees realize the OEO has full backing from the top. To ensure that this involvement really takes place, the Task Force recommends that the Corporation take three actions:

46. Create equal opportunity committees at each of the corporate, divisional, and regional levels.

The equal opportunity committees that we are recommending are intended to provide a vehicle for senior managers to participate in the equal opportunity program. The committees should meet semiannually to review achievements, agree on further steps to be taken in the next 6 months, and approve a timetable. At the corporate level, the committee should consist of the President and Executive Vice-President; the divisional Vice-President - General Managers; the Vice-President, Human Resources; and the Director of the OEO. Divisionally, the committees would consist of the VP-GM and AGM, the Director of Human Resources, and the equal opportunity officer. Regionally, the Regional Director, the media directors, the personnel manager, and the equal opportunity representative would form the committee.

47. Report annually to the CBC's Board of Directors on progress in the equal opportunity program.

This regular report would serve the purpose not only of keeping the Board members informed of progress, but also of reminding senior management that results are expected. As new people enter senior management, this practice should also help to ensure continuity of interest and involvement.

48. Include pressing equal opportunity items on the agendas of regular senior management meetings.

Such items might include the approval of extra funds to meet unforeseen costs on an action project, or a sensitive matter raised by a women's group. These would appear only occasionally, as required, on the agenda of the Joint Management Committee at the corporate level, and meetings of senior officers at the divisional level.

ACCOUNTABILITY

As a final requirement for implementation, it is essential that line managers be held responsible for results; this can best be done by building accountability formally into their annual objectives. Then there can be no misunderstanding; everyone will know that senior management wants action, and will have a clear understanding of just what is expected. Besides getting a down-the-line commitment to specific objectives, it will permit measurement of the results. Thus, the Task Force recommends that the Corporation:

49. Set annual equal opportunity objectives down to the level of large locations.

The objectives set would rarely be quantitative. That is, most objectives, at least in the first years, would be in the form of projects, so that numerical goals would seldom be set. For example, the objectives for the director of one region might read:

1. By July 1, establish the selection board system for all vacancies, as outlined in the Task Force report.

2. Make available full-time personnel and the necessary funds to work on secretarial compensation and career path projects.

Numerical goals would be reserved for a few cases only. They might, for example, be set for very large organizational units, such as the entire English Services division, and might take the form of a statement that "ESD will seek to increase the proportion of women in management by X percentage points over the next 2 years". Numerical goals might also be set in the case of a subordinate manager who voluntarily proposes a target for his own location: e.g., "In this region, we believe it is reasonable for us to have two more MS women by the year-end". Targets of this kind might also be envisaged where a severe problem exists (as in regions that have no women in management and no women as producers), and where voluntary action has not improved the situation over a period of 1 to 2 years. In other words, we are in favour of specific objectives backed up by positive action, but not of quotas.

The objectives would be set from the corporate level right down to location level (Figure 102), with the President and Executive Vice-President setting overall corporate objectives; the VPs setting objectives for their corporate staff; and so on down the line.

CONCLUSION

Implementing a program to ensure equal opportunity for women is, as we have said, a complex venture, and it will take at least 3 to 4 years to achieve all its aims. What, then, are the chances of success for the program we have recommended?

The Task Force believes they are very good, provided that senior management is really committed to action. Two particular circumstances in the Corporation at the present time encourage us to be optimistic, and the experience of other organizations with equal opportunity programs also suggests that it is possible to achieve significant results - again provided that top management takes a continuing and genuine interest.

The first internal reason for optimism is the wide variation between situations at different locations. Some locations have already managed to reduce the gulf between the two sexes, and have shown that it is possible to desegregate jobs without a loss in either the quality or the quantity of the programs that are our raison d'être. By way of example, Figure 103 illustrates the difference between Ottawa Area and Winnipeg. Figure 23 (page 39) also demonstrates the wide variations among different centres in the proportion of women in management. Our conclusion is that if one location can narrow the gap between men and women, there is no reason why other centres cannot do the same.
No reason, that is, if there is enough expansion and turnover in the staff to allow for change. Here, in the Corporation as a whole, the prospects in the next few years are better than they have been in the past. As we pointed out in Chapter 3, there will be many vacancies between now and 1980; taking the number of people who will be retiring, and adding a figure based on normal turnover, we find that over 4,000 jobs will be open. On top of that, the planned expansion to reach areas of the country not now receiving full CBC coverage will create an additional 4,000 jobs. Many of these jobs are in

LEVELS FOR WHICH WRITTEN OBJECTIVES EXIST

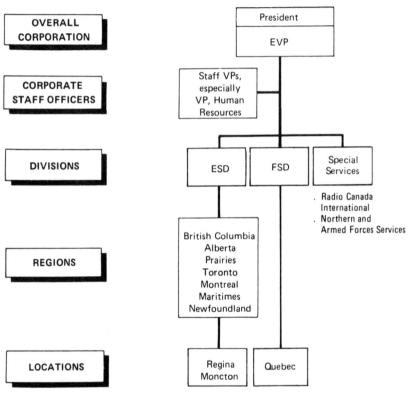

Fig. 102   Objectives would be set from the corporate level down to the location level

COMPARISONS OF GAPS
BETWEEN MEN AND WOMEN

AREA		MEASURE	SITUATION	
			Ottawa Area	Winnipeg
Salaries		Percentage women less than men	25.0	32.0
Training		Percentage difference between proportion of women and men trained	18.0	3,100.00
Advancement		Percentage difference between women's representation on staff and share of advancements	0.0	(4.0)
Power	MS	Percentage women's representation in position category	2.9	3.6
	TV Producer		12.5	0.0
	Radio Producer		37.5	14.4
	News		9.7	8.0
	Film		6.7	0.0

Fig. 103 Significant variation among locations suggests that improvement is possible

181

management and other key positions. In short - especially if the CBC embarks on an active recruiting program, and encourages schools and universities to prepare women for the wide variety of careers in the Corporation - there is no reason why the present segregation should not have been completely broken down by the 1980s.

The record of other organizations that have decided to take steps to ensure equality of treatment (Figure 104) is another basis for optimism. A major Canadian bank increased the percentage of women in management almost threefold in the 4-year period from 1969 to 1973. A Crown Corporation with an affirmative action program increased the number of female economists from 8.7 percent to 14.3 percent between 1970 and 1974; in the same time span, it also saw women in senior administrative positions go from 1.9 percent to 5.3 percent, and the numbers of women acting as administrative assistants jumped from 9 percent to 27 percent. A major U.S. broadcasting organization listed women as receiving 41.1 percent of all promotions in the first quarter of 1973; just over a year later, in the second quarter of 1974, they received 53.9 percent of all promotions.

In conclusion, we believe the implementation of the equal opportunity program should now be given a very high priority. We have already stressed the many ways in which we believe that the CBC as well as its employees would benefit internally, with improved morale, better use of all employees' talents, and a new impetus to improve training and career planning. We also believe that this is a major opportunity for the CBC (Figure 105); an opportunity both to anticipate forthcoming federal human rights legislation, which will forbid discrimination in employment, and to place itself in a position of leadership among Canadian enterprises, rather than the middle position in which it now finds itself (Figure 106).

These are among the many valid reasons for the CBC to act with energy and determination to implement the recommendations put forward in this report. But the most compelling reason of all is simply this: **IT IS THE RIGHT THING TO DO.**

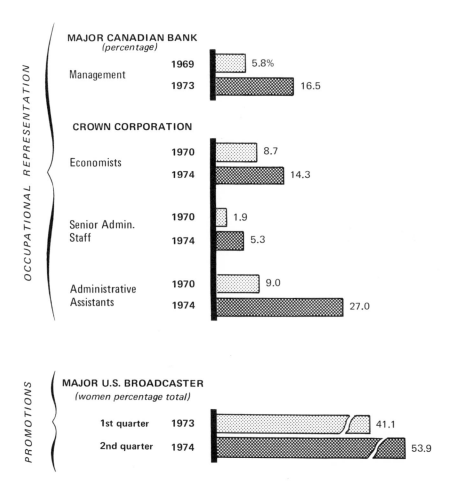

MAJOR CANADIAN BANK
(percentage)

Management
- 1969 — 5.8%
- 1973 — 16.5

CROWN CORPORATION

Economists
- 1970 — 8.7
- 1974 — 14.3

Senior Admin. Staff
- 1970 — 1.9
- 1974 — 5.3

Administrative Assistants
- 1970 — 9.0
- 1974 — 27.0

MAJOR U.S. BROADCASTER
(women percentage total)

- 1st quarter 1973 — 41.1
- 2nd quarter 1974 — 53.9

OCCUPATIONAL REPRESENTATION

PROMOTIONS

Fig. 104   Equal opportunity programs in other organizations have been successful

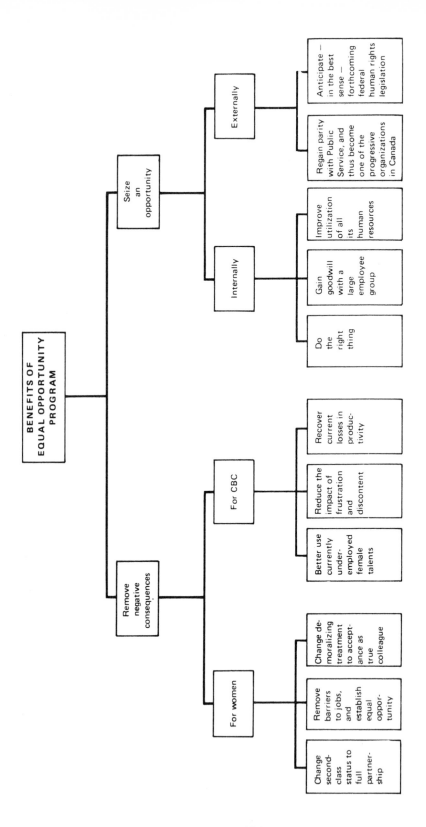

Fig. 105 The recommended program will benefit both the CBC and its
employees, and provides the Corporation with a major opportunity

184

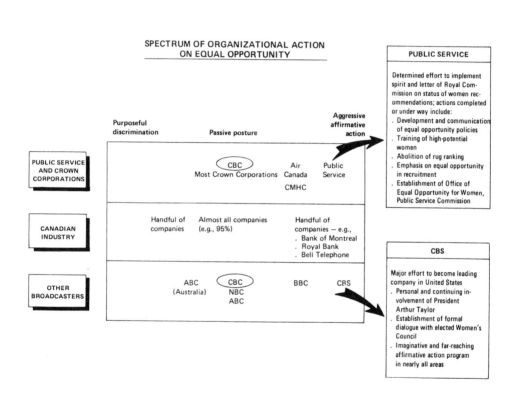

SPECTRUM OF ORGANIZATIONAL ACTION
ON EQUAL OPPORTUNITY

Purposeful discrimination

Passive posture

Aggressive affirmative action

PUBLIC SERVICE AND CROWN CORPORATIONS

CBC
Most Crown Corporations
Air Canada
CMHC
Public Service

CANADIAN INDUSTRY

Handful of companies
Almost all companies (e.g., 95%)
Handful of companies — e.g.,
. Bank of Montreal
. Royal Bank
. Bell Telephone

OTHER BROADCASTERS

ABC (Australia)
CBC
NBC
ABC
BBC
CBS

PUBLIC SERVICE

Determined effort to implement spirit and letter of Royal Commission on status of women recommendations; actions completed or under way include:
. Development and communication of equal opportunity policies
. Training of high-potential women
. Abolition of rug ranking
. Emphasis on equal opportunity in recruitment
. Establishment of Office of Equal Opportunity for Women, Public Service Commission

CBS

Major effort to become leading company in United States
. Personal and continuing involvement of President Arthur Taylor
. Establishment of formal dialogue with elected Women's Council
. Imaginative and far-reaching affirmative action program in nearly all areas

Fig. 106   Today, the CBC is in a middle position on equal opportunity

185

MANAGEMENT RESPONSE

The Task Force has made eight recommendations to ensure effective implementation of the overall equal opportunity program. We accept seven in full and one in part.

Staff Support

42. Undertake a long-term equal opportunity program, which would phase in the recommended changes over a period of 3 to 4 years.
Accepted in full.

43. Create an Office of Equal Opportunity (OEO) and direct it to give top priority to implementing the program to ensure equal opportunity for women in the CBC.
Accepted in full. We would stress in particular the Task Force's point that the OEO's mission is to implement the recommendations contained in this report, and *not* to act as an ombudsman or commission that follows up complaints of discrimination by individual employees.

44. Establish the following positions within the OEO, reporting to the senior human resources manager; at the corporate level, a Director reporting to the Vice President, Human Resources, and supported by two co-ordinators and a research analyst; in each division, an equal opportunity officer who reports to the Director, Human Resources; in each region, an equal opportunity representative, who may be full- or part-time, and who reports to the senior personnel officer.
Accepted, subject to later approval of the Office's precise organization structure. This recommendation has two important components, each of which requires a separate response.

First, we agree that at each level of the organization the senior equal opportunity position should report to the senior human resources officer; namely, the Vice President, Human Resources at the corporate level, the Director, Human Resources in each division, and the Personnel and Administration Manager at large locations or in separate units such as Radio-Canada International and Engineering Headquarters.

Second, we believe that the specific positions that the Task Force recommends for each level of the organization represent approximately the appropriate level and type of capability. However, before giving final approval, we would like to see a more complete organizational plan that spells out such details as the precise responsibilities for each job, the specific projects on which the new incumbents would work for the first year, and descriptions of how these individuals would work with line and personnel managers. As we see it, this sort of plan is required to ensure that the Equal Opportunity Office gets off to a fully effective start.

45. Staff the OEO using the selection board process.
Accepted in full.

Senior Management Involvement

46. Create equal opportunity committees at each of the corporate, divisional, and regional levels.
Accepted in full.

47. Report annually to the CBC's Board of Directors on progress in the equal opportunity program.
Accepted in full.

Accountability in the Line

48. Include pressing equal opportunity items on the agendas of regular senior management meetings.
Accepted in full.

49. Set annual equal opportunity objectives down to the level of large locations.
Accepted in full.

APPENDIX 1 — ADDITIONAL ISSUES

This appendix contains the five issues that were peripheral to the Task Force's main activity. Two of the issues are indeed closely related to the status of women but were not, strictly speaking, within our mandate. These are sexism in programming and in commercials, and the status of women on contract. The three other issues, while they certainly affect women, seemed to us to have an equal bearing on the careers of men. They are training, job counselling, and an "ombudsman" function.

Sexism in Programming

Many people throughout the country voiced their disappointment that the Task Force could not deal directly with the question of sexism in programming - that is, the distorted or stereotyped image of women that many feel is projected by the CBC in its programming, especially on television. Many women believe that this issue is just as important as equal opportunity in their work; they are embarrassed that their employer should continue to program on the basis of a cliché that encourages society to "keep women in their place", by showing them as "silly harebrained mantraps", or "worried drudges whose nightmare is a kitchen floor that does not shine like a mirror". Further, they point out that the media have enormous power to shape society's view of women, and believe that the CBC, as a public broadcaster, has a special responsibility to reflect reality.

The Task Force believes that this subject is sufficiently important to deserve a separate examination. For one thing, the CBC does not itself produce everything that emanates from its screens, nor can it at present afford to do so. In addition, one would have not only to assess what is inaccurate and distasteful, but also to study the impact on revenue and on audiences of refusing to broadcast material that might be considered offensive.

In the long term, as the equal opportunity program recommended by the Task Force brings more women into senior programming jobs and important on-air functions, much of what is now unacceptable may well disappear. But this will take time, and other kinds of action are also needed. We believe that the CBC should establish more clear-cut commercial acceptance policies and guidelines, and that it should spearhead an awareness throughout the industry of the need for change. Therefore, the Task Force recommends that the Corporation:

> 50. **Determine the extent of sexism in CBC programs, and work with program personnel to develop a policy statement on program standards.**
>
> 51. **Establish more clear-cut commercial acceptance guidelines.**

52. Alert outside sources of broadcast material to CBC policies with regard to the portrayal of women.

Women on Contract

Women on contract, and those who make their living doing freelance work for the CBC on an ad hoc basis, have special problems. The majority of those we heard from are convinced that they are being taken advantage of in matters of pay, and that they are limited in their assignments to "women's topics" or "kooky stories". While it was not within our province to follow up these charges, the complaints were so widespread that they could not be ignored; accordingly, as a starting point, Recommendation 29, in the Compensation section (page 125) was that the Corporation *conduct a separate examination of the pay of contract personnel.*

Should such a study find the charges to be based on fact, further work might be required. Producers have jurisdiction over the hiring of freelancers for their programs, and it would be necessary not only to issue a policy statement for them to refer to, but also to develop guidelines to ensure that they apply these policies in making assignments.

Training

CBC staff across the country told the Task Force that training is inadequate. Their views support the general conclusion of the CBC/McKinsey human resources management study that lack of training is a serious problem. Two other points also emerged: many employees, particularly women, were not aware of training courses that are now available; and the training problem seems to be much less serious in locations with a full-time staff training officer, as in the Ottawa Area.

In the area of training, then, the Task Force recommends that the Corporation:

53. Issue a memorandum to all staff, clarifying current training policies and describing existing training programs.

54. Establish the position of a full-time training officer in all locations with over 200 employees; in the smaller locations, designate a training coordinator.

Job Counselling

A very large proportion of the employees we spoke to expressed a need for individual job counselling. Many simply have no idea what career opportunities exist; others have expectations that are bound to be frustrated, either because of a lack of openings in the areas they want to enter, or because their estimates of their own capabilities and qualifications for such jobs are unrealistic. Over and over we heard the same thing: *"There's no one to go to for help or advice".*

One difficulty in dealing with this need is that, at present, the position of job counsellor would be an almost impossible one. Before effective counsel can be given, certain steps must be taken. There must be a systematic study to identify the job categories and locations where a significant number of vacancies will or will not arise. Career paths must be identified - and developed, where none exist. And means must be found to measure the potential of individual employees.

Accomplishing these things will take time. The new human resources management program will not be in full swing for several months, and even then a good deal of staff work will be involved in developing career paths and doing other necessary preparatory work.

So, with respect to job counselling, the Task Force recommends that the Corporation:

> **55. Undertake to provide job counselling as part of the overall human resources management improvement program.**

Ombudsman Function

Under present circumstances, some employees need a "court of appeal" when they believe that they have been dealt with unfairly by the Corporation. Union employees may have complaints that are not covered by their agreements, although in the main the union employee is in a strong position, since he or she can call in a union officer as advocate. Confidential and supervisory employees, however, feel that they have no recourse, and many expressed the need for a person or body to whom they could appeal. Ideally, the Personnel Manager should fulfill this role, except when the complaint arises in his or her own department. Appealing to the "boss's boss" is also accepted practice, but this route is often felt to be unproductive, since the "top boss" may not be willing to interfere with the supervisor's authority. Or, in cases of discrimination, for instance, both may hold similar views.

An ombudsman, almost by definition, has total independence and objectivity. We recognize the difficulties that might arise from setting up such an office outside the personnel structures. However, if no action is taken, this function might easily fall to the Office of Equal Opportunity. Since the OEO should spend its time on implementation of major programs to benefit large groups of people, rather than acting on behalf of individuals, we believe this would be misuse of the Office.

Under the circumstances, the Task Force recommends that the Corporation:

> **56. Request the Vice President, Human Resources, to formulate a plan for establishing an ombudsman capability for CBC employees.**

★ ★ ★ ★ ★

MANAGEMENT RESPONSE

In this chapter, the Task Force has made seven recommendations in four separate areas. Although these areas are, strictly speaking, outside the group's mandate, we have responded to them because of the importance of the issues they address.

Sexism on Air

> **50. Determine the extent of sexism in CBC programs, and work with program personnel to develop a policy statement on program standards.**

> **51. Establish more clear-cut commercial acceptance guidelines.**

> **52. Alert outside sources of broadcast material to CBC policies with regard to the portrayal of women.**

> We have noted the Task Force's observations, and acknowledge that there is some concern surrounding these questions. However, the basic issue is a matter of program policy, which calls for more detailed study and consideration before any formal corporate undertaking can be made. The Task Force's observations are therefore being referred to our Program Policy group, which will be looking into this question.

Training and Job Counselling

> **53. Issue a memorandum to all staff, clarifying current training policies and describing existing training programs.**

> **54. Establish the position of a full-time training officer in all locations with over 200 employees; in the smaller locations, designate a training coordinator.**

> **55. Undertake to provide job counselling as part of the overall human resources management improvement program.**

> The Corporation agrees in principle with the three recommendations made by the Task Force in the area of training and job counselling. However, the timing and method of their implementation will be dealt with as part of the Corporation's broader reorientation of human resources management, to which several allusions have already been made in the Task Force report and recommendations.

Ombudsman Capability

56. Request the Vice-President, Human Resources, to formulate a plan for establishing an ombudsman capability for CBC employees.

Not accepted. We are most sympathetic to the need of employees for an avenue of appeal when they believe they have been treated unfairly, and either cannot go to their supervisor because the supervisor is part of the problem, or have consulted the supervisor and obtained little satisfaction. At present, there are two such avenues: the union to which the employee belongs and the personnel officer at his or her location.

Now it may be that today neither of these is fully effective, so that many employees do not obtain the hearing they seek. However, we do *not* believe that the creation of yet another avenue - an ombudsman capability of some sort - is the solution to the problem, for by its very nature, the ombudsman role is one that "interferes" with established mechanisms for handling problems and often causes more difficulty than it resolves.

Indeed, if we in the Corporation cannot make the existing, more traditional avenues work properly, there is little prospect that we will be able to make a success of a delicate organizational creature such as an ombudsman.

Thus, we cannot accept the recommendation made by the Task Force. However, as part of the overall human resources program, we do commit the Corporation to upgrading the personnel function's ability to handle the problems of individual employees. Further, we stand ready to cooperate fully with the CBC's unions in initiatives they may wish to take to strengthen the ways in which they deal with the problems of their membership. And, we will, of course, keep a close watch on the Corporation's progress in making existing vehicles more effective. Should this improvement be slower than expected we will be prepared to reconsider the situation.

APPENDIX 2   -   SUMMARY OF RECOMMENDATIONS

JOB ACCESS

1.   Develop and communicate throughout the Corporation an equal opportunity policy with detailed guidelines for its implementation.

2.   Revise all recruitment materials to eliminate sex stereotyping.

3.   Communicate new equal opportunity policy to all major sources of outside candidates for employment.

4.   Ensure that all external employment advertising invites both men and women applicants.

5.   Work with unions to remove - where practical - sex from position titles.

6.   Revise application forms to remove questions on sex and marital status, and encourage use of initials rather than first names.

7.   Redesign notice of vacancy form to include invitation to both men and women applicants.

8.   Develop new interview guidelines and circulate to all employment personnel and supervisors.

9.   Post all jobs up to and including MS V.

10.   Have manpower planning personnel, working with the Office of Equal Opportunity, develop an inventory of women, to be consulted by decision makers.

11.   Establish selection boards for all vacancies from above lowest entry level up to and including MS V.

12.   Ensure that awareness sessions are built into the supervisory training program that is being developed in 1975/76.

13.   Conduct pilot awareness sessions outside supervisory training, using professional resources; extend these sessions across the CBC if they are successful.

14.   Develop and implement affirmative action programs to increase the proportion of women in management and other key jobs, and to break down segregation by sex in positions at lower levels.

15.   Carry out the action programs on a decentralized basis, working with senior managers.

16.   Monitor, through the Office of Equal Opportunity, progress both in the Corporation as a whole, and in individual locations.

17.   Present, through the Office of Equal Opportunity, regular reports to management on the progress - or lack of progress - in the matter of job access in the Corporation as a whole and in individual locations; and issue an annual report to all employees.

SECRETARIES

18.   Establish an action program that gives special encouragement to qualified secretaries to advance into administration and production.

19.   Undertake, as a first step, a project in an English Services region outside Toronto to design and implement new advancement paths.

20.   Abolish rug ranking, and institute instead a job evaluation plan for stenographers and secretaries.

21.   Use the project team approach for designing and implementing the plan, working at the same English Services location as for the advancement project.

22.   Develop detailed job descriptions for secretaries, starting with the English Services pilot project.

23.   Seek to increase the number of men engaged in secretarial functions.

24.   Ensure that a session on boss-secretary relationships is incorporated in supervisory training.

COMPENSATION

25.   Develop and distribute to all employees an overall equal pay policy and guidelines for its administration.

26.   Request, following the issuance of that policy, that all supervisors review the salaries of men and women in identical position categories, to determine whether differences are justified.

27.   Review annually all entry salaries and position-by-position comparisons, and follow up apparent anomalies with the supervisors concerned.

28.   Incorporate materials on unconscious discrimination in salary administration into general supervisory training.

29.   Conduct a separate examination of the pay of contract personnel.

30.   Equalize coverage under the Group Life Plan, within 9 months.

31. Investigate the possibility of a later revision of the plan to introduce optional coverage.

32. Equalize survivor benefits.

33. Investigate the possibility of broadening the definition of dependents to that used in the Income Tax Act, with the understanding that only one adult could be named as a dependent, along with dependent children as presently defined.

34. Implement immediately the Corporate Personnel revision of the definition of "dependents" in the Northern Allowance policy.

35. Change all references from "wife" to "spouse" in both policy and forms that describe Transfer and Removal Allowances.

RESPONSIBILITIES OF PARENTHOOD

36. Establish, for employees with 1 year of service or more, a separate paid paternity leave, to be included in an overall birth policy.

37. Set the leave entitlement at 3 days.

38. Pay, for women with a minimum of 1 year's service, full salary and the Corporation's share of benefit costs during maternity leave for a period of up to 15 weeks, to be taken at her discretion, provided she signifies her intention to return.

39. Guarantee the new mother the identical position upon her return.

40. Undertake to provide assistance to employees in obtaining improved child care facilities.

41. Undertake, as a first step, a feasibility study in Montreal to determine what form the assistance should take.

OVERALL ACTION PROGRAM

42. Undertake a long-term equal opportunity program, which would phase in the recommended changes over a period of 3 to 4 years.

43. Create an Office of Equal Opportunity (OEO) and direct it to give top priority to implementing the program to ensure equal opportunity for women in the CBC.

44. Establish the following positions within the OEO, reporting to the senior human resources manager:

    — At the corporate level, a Director reporting to the Vice-President, Human Resources, and supported by two coordinators and a research analyst

- In each division, an equal opportunity officer who reports to the Director, Human Resources

- In each region, an equal opportunity representative, who may be full- or part-time, and who reports to the senior personnel officer.

45. Staff the OEO using the selection board process.

46. Create equal opportunity committees at each of the corporate, divisional, and regional levels.

47. Report annually to the CBC's Board of Directors on progress in the equal opportunity program.

48. Include pressing equal opportunity items on the agendas of regular senior management meetings.

49. Set annual equal opportunity objectives down to the level of large locations.

ADDITIONAL ISSUES

50. Determine the extent of sexism in CBC programs, and work with program personnel to develop a policy statement on program standards.

51. Establish more clear-cut commercial acceptance guidelines.

52. Alert outside sources of broadcast material to CBC policies with regard to the portrayal of women.

53. Issue a memorandum to all staff, clarifying current training policies and describing existing training programs.

54. Establish the position of a full-time training officer in all locations with over 200 employees; in the smaller locations, designate a training coordinator.

55. Undertake to provide job counselling as part of the overall human resources management improvement program.

56. Request the Vice-President, Human Resources, to formulate a plan for establishing an ombudsman capability for CBC employees.